MW00772171

FROM COTTAGE TO WORK STATION

ALLAN CARLSON

FROM COTTAGE
TO WORK STATION

*The Family's Search for
Social Harmony in the Industrial Age*

RARE CHRISTIAN BOOKS
19275 Highway 28
Dixon, MO 65459
Ph./Fax: (573) 336-7316

IGNATIUS PRESS   SAN FRANCISCO

Cover by Riz Boncan Marsella

©1993 Ignatius Press, San Francisco
ISBN 0-89870-429-4
Library of Congress catalogue number 92-74569
Printed in the United States of America

Contents

To Anders, Sarah-Eva, Anna, and Miriam

Foreword

Allan Carlson's book *From Cottage to Work Station* considers, within the modern era, the types of economic support a human family needs to be itself and to foster its primary purpose. The book thus bears the explanatory subtitle "The Family's Search for Social Harmony in the Industrial Age". Some basic conflict between social harmony and industry in its many forms has been at the forefront of politics and economics, even into the computer and information age. Carlson traces the nature of this conflict, the efforts to meet it, and its intrinsic dynamics when the very meaning of the family comes to be questioned or even rejected.

At first sight, this book will seem like a massive, yet fascinating, accumulation of particular details and data about family history and structure, about industrial organization, about religion, army, unions, and households. Yet, as one reads on, it will become more and more evident that this study is not merely a record of a remarkable, even ominous, change in our understanding of the family. It is also a theoretical analysis of the reasons for this change and a positive proposal about how we must rethink this fundamental institution and particularly those economic ideas, initiatives, and institutions that are designed to support it.

In Aristotle, the family — the household — was not the state, though its members were in preparation to become members or, if already adults, to participate in it. The most basic things of life were within the mystery of the household. Life was conceived, begun, and nurtured here. The daily sustenance of life took place here, not merely food and clothing, but moral growth and guidance. The household was, in one sense, the area of necessity, of the things that had to be done if life is to exist at all. Death, too, most often took place here, when not on the battlefield or by accident. The transcendent mysteries of human life are most evident here in the family, even though the polity was also necessary to complete and perfect this very human life already begun in the family.

For the highest things, both household and polity were needed, but the highest things were also beyond politics. Politics was limited by the contemplative order. The household, on the other hand, was supported by property. Aristotle recognized that a certain amount of material goods was necessary for the sustenance of life and for virtue. The very word *liberal* meant generosity with one's goods, not being dominated by wealth or property in one's purpose in life. We needed goods and revealed our souls in what we did with them. Economics had the purpose of sustaining life, but the life of the household itself was not merely its material provisions, however necessary these were.

Aristotle, of course, developed his thesis as a direct result of a famous proposal in Plato's *Republic* about the communality of wives, children, and property. This common ownership, or communality, was, it was said, the best and necessary condition for the philosophic guardians in any polity. Certain modern writers maintain that Plato was not intending that this proposal, replete with genetic engineering and the destruction of the family in the name of some higher good, was to be taken literally. It was designed rather to caution utopian philosophers against overturning the normal limits of fallible and normal mankind, against, in fact, tampering with the family.

Aristotle himself, however, took this proposal about the communality of wives, children, and property seriously. Aristotle, in the second book of *The Politics,* argued very carefully with Plato about the feasibility of these proposals. He thought that communality of wives and children was exactly what we did not want. The whole meaning of love and friendship was to have particular, lifetime relationships with specific individuals. It was better to be Plato's actual cousin than his communal "brother" in a system in which no one recognized his own father or mother or relatives. Aristotle maintained that property would not be at all well taken care of in a communal ownership and that human initiative would be subverted in such a system.

I bring these classical references up because, in reading Carlson's modern history of the family, it will become clear that this classic controversy, in one form or another, is at work in the evolution of family policy. We find proposals for putting children in day-care centers and women in the army or in the work force not unlike Plato's proposal was in its purity. Of course, the forms in which these ideas are prevalent have differed over time and place, but from Australia to Sweden, France, England, Germany, and the United States, this very struggle about the centrality and normalcy of the family and its supports is at work, as this book details.

Carlson has recognized that certain otherwise valid economic ideas of competition or efficiency can, when applied to the family, weaken or destroy it. He also knows that the family is not only a spiritual or moral entity, but also one that needs a grounding in goods and products and responsibility for houses and neighborhoods and, yes, education. No doubt, one of the most fascinating aspects of this study is its documentation of the problems and controversies caused by persistent efforts to support the family—housing policy, military family policy, home economics courses, family wage policies. Carlson, a most intelligent supporter of full family life, is not afraid to trace how efforts conceived with the best of intentions can work against the health or structure of the family.

From Cottage to Work Station is a sobering book. Allan Carlson recognizes that individualist and communist philosophies in differing ways undermine the unique nature of the family. He also indicates the beginnings of studies that are showing the dramatic and drastic consequences of politics and attitudes that seek to replace or undermine the family. This effort to understand what is going on with regard to the centrality of the family in civilized life requires a reconsideration of feminism, nontraditional family units, delinquency, health, divorce, and the many other problems that have arisen in a society that has not understood either the meaning of the family or what is required to support its uniqueness.

Carlson also shows how religious thinking about the family in all the major religions is also considerably engaged in and affected by current controversies over what a family is and how it is to be supported. He maintains that religion is directly related to family life, yet is not sufficient for it without proper economic and political support. But Carlson is also acutely aware that many strands of religious thinking have followed the ideas and practices that have been destructive of family life.

To write accurately about the family today is, then, a most sobering task and for that reason, no doubt, a most necessary one. In this reflective, incisive study by Allan Carlson, the clear outlines of the problems and their origins are found in a way no one else has treated so accurately. The precise description and defense of the family are the most essential acts of civilization in the next decade and next century. Carlson maintains, as Aristotle did, that we must return to a clear and proper understanding of our families and the household goods and properties that make the family not only possible but flourishing. In this sense, this is not a happy book because too much is wrong with the family. But it is, in another sense, a hopeful book because someone with the perception of Allan Carlson has begun the difficult work of showing in detail what has gone wrong and what might make it right.

James V. Schall, S.J.
Professor, Department of Government
Georgetown University

Introduction: The Broken Home

The introduction of machine technology and the factory system of production forced the reordering of Western social life beginning during the nineteenth century. Prior to their appearance, the daily flow of events for the vast majority of the European peoples had been surprisingly stable. For over a millennium, householding had been the dominant economic pattern, with production for trade a relatively minor feature. Residence and workplace were normally one and the same, whether in the form of a farmer's cottage or a craftsman's shop. Household production, ranging from tool making and weaving to the keeping of livestock and the garden patch, bound each family together as a basic economic unit, a "community of work."[1] Production complemented consumption and made the family largely self-sufficient, albeit at a relatively mean level of existence. Wives and children stood beside husbands and fathers as coworkers in the family enterprise, with no debate over issues of work and dependency.[2] Indeed, family living was so central to life itself that it was largely taken for granted, being the social equivalent of breathing. Well into the nineteenth century, markets and money were of limited importance to the average farmer, cottager, or craftsman. In the European countryside, a varied mix of feudal obligations, payments-in-kind, barter, subsistence agriculture, and market production dominated.[3] In towns, labor was governed by an elaborate series

[1] John Demos, *Past, Present, and Personal: The Family and the Life Course in American History* (New York: Oxford University Press, 1986), 28.

[2] See Ivy Pinchbeck, *Women Workers and the Industrial Revolution, 1750–1850* (London: George Routledge and Sons, 1930), 7–26.

[3] On this general subject, see Heinrich Slicher van Bath, *The Agrarian History of Western Europe, A.D. 500–1850,* trans. Olive Ordish (London: Edward Arnold, 1963).

1

of customs and regulations designed, in part, to preserve the dignity of workers and the autonomy of households.

Industrialization tore asunder this settled, family-oriented European world. In historian John Demos' words: "Family life was wrenched apart from the world of work—a veritable sea-change in social history."[4] The goods produced by factories using a division of labor rapidly displaced household-produced commodities such as cloth, shoes, and candles. The unique demands of the new machines, the construction of factories, and the need for labor discipline further severed the workplace from the home. In the new economic order, family living quickly ceased to have a dominant productive side. Family units tended to reorganize as places for shared consumption and shelter. Through legal changes abolishing the protections of rural tradition and guild privileges, labor became a commodity governed for the first time by a national, and eventually an international, market. The reciprocal, complementary tasks of husbands and wives in household production were quickly leveled, and questions grew about gender roles in the new order. Older children, too, could forego the obedience demanded by lineage and birth and sell their own labor to manufacturers. In the industrial milieu, the inward-looking, autonomous, cooperative family changed into a collection of individuals in potential, and often real, competition with each other. As residual dependents, infants and small children had no immediate prospects for individual economic gain; the market mechanism left their fate uncertain.

This common story of change defined the terrain for the great ideological battles of the nineteenth century. Protests against the distortion of the old ways and the severance of labor from home were penned by Friedrich Engels, Robert Owen, and others. Popular movements emerged, such as Chartism in England and the 1847–48 artisans' revolt in Germany, followed by the blossoming of socialist theory among the intellectuals.

---

[4] Demos, *Past, Present, and Personal,* p. 32.

Also stimulated by these startling changes, classical economic theory took form in the work of T. R. Malthus, David Ricardo, John Stuart Mill, and Alfred Marshall. The rise of labor unions, the clash of economic interests, and the political disorders that followed were other consequences of the swift change from a household economy to an industrial economy, what philosopher Karl Polanyi has called "The Great Transformation".[5]

Americans, though, have had little sense of this historical pageant. At least since the appearance of Alexis de Tocqueville's *Democracy in America,* the operative assumptions have been that the United States was born modern in a commitment to change and progress, that democracy and a commercialized economy have always defined the American experiment, and that the disruptive separation of workplace from home has never been a major American issue. This French observer described the spirit guiding the United States in the 1830s as fundamentally progressive and idealistic: "When castes disappear and classes are brought together, when men are jumbled together and habits, customs, and laws are changing, when new facts impinge and new truths are discovered, when old conceptions vanish and new ones take their place, then the human mind imagines the possibility of an ideal but always fugitive perfection." Concerning American occupations, he argued that agriculture was a fading reality and that "almost all the tastes and habits born of equality naturally led men in the direction of trade and industry."[6] A corollary to these contentions has been that Americans have been singularly blessed with an avoidance of the conflicts that have shaken Europeans. Struggles by national labor movements to defend family life, social intervention to save the family economy, the use of nationalism as a pretext for a new social solidarity — these all have a faintly alien, un-

---

[5] Karl Polanyi, *The Great Transformation* (Boston: Beacon Press, 1944).

[6] Alexis de Tocqueville, *Democracy in America,* ed. J. P. Mayer (Garden City, NY: Anchor Books, 1969), 453, 551.

American odor and seem to be the by-products of Europe's more fitful history.

This volume begins with a different perspective on the American social past. It rests on the contention that the United States was founded as a premodern nation, on the assumption that autonomous households rooted in land and lineage would be the social and economic base of national life. This treatise also argues that the social effect of industrialization—particularly the great divorce of labor from the home—has been one of the defining factors in American domestic life since the 1840s as well as the source of numerous projects to limit or divert commercial progress and so heal the divide between work and family. Finally, the volume shows that for most of the twentieth century, Americans have continued to experiment with strategies to heal this basic breech. As contemporary public policy disputes over parental leave, day-care funding, and educational goals suggest, the tension between family and work still remains among the central social issues in American life.

There are several premises that should be acknowledged at the outset. First, I hold that the family is the natural, universal, and irreplaceable human community. Understood as a man and a woman in a socially approved bond for the purposes of sharing intimacy and resources and propagating and rearing children, the family also exists as the conservator of lineage and tradition. It ties the living to the legacy of the past and gives them a proper consciousness of the future. With Pierre Guillaume and Frederic LePlay, I maintain that the family "by a remarkable favor of Providence has within its very structure the beneficent qualities of the individual and those of association". Such family living, in turn, rests ideally on the ownership of the homestead, solid habits of work, adherence to inherited mores, internal self-reliance in crisis, and fecundity. [7]

Second, I maintain that it is out of the reciprocal life of the

---

[7] Pierre Guillaume and Frederic LePlay, *Le Reform Sociale,* vol. 1, bk. 3 (Tours: A. Mame et fils, 1887), chaps. 24–30.

family that broader communities grow: tribes, villages, peoples, nations. This view is congruent with the work of LePlay, Carle Zimmerman, and Pitirim Sorokin in emphasizing the organic status of the family as the "cell of society".[8]

Some find the universality of the family to be a matter explained spiritually, as the pattern of human social life ordained or blessed by God.[9] Others trace the same phenomenon to the foundations of human biology, through the genetic inheritance found in human DNA.[10] Still others find this universality validated through social research, which both identifies the family as an anthropological norm and traces specific social disorders to a common source in the breakdown of the family.[11] I presume that all three understandings are encompassed by a vision of both the natural world and human nature as ordered — morally, socially, and physically — by a common intelligence, with each sphere properly reflecting that shared origin.

These premises mean that I see divergences from this family order as a falling away from the universal model rather than merely as change. From this perspective, the family as defined here is not a malleable instrument in the service of history, but rather a constant expectation for all humanity, past, present, and future. Moreover, observers can properly gauge the social

[8] Carle Zimmerman and Merle Frampton, *Family and Society: A Study of the Sociology of Reconstruction* (New York: D. Van Nostrand, 1935); Pitirim Sorokin and Carle Zimmerman, *Principles of Rural-Urban Sociology* (New York: Henry Holt and Company, 1929), 233; and Pitirim Sorokin, *The Crisis of Our Age* (New York: E. P. Dutton, 1941), 167.

[9] The Roman Catholic perspective is best displayed in the encyclicals *Quanta Cura* (1864), *Rerum Novarum* (1891), *Casti Connubii* (1933), and *Humanae Vitae* (1968). The Protestant understanding of family life as divinely ordained receives able analysis in Steven Ozment, *When Fathers Ruled: Family Life in Reformation Europe* (Cambridge, MA: Harvard University Press, 1983).

[10] For the best elaboration of this argument, see Thomas Fleming, *The Politics of Human Nature* (New Brunswick, NJ: Transaction Books, 1988), chaps. 4, 5.

[11] As example, see Pitirim A. Sorokin, *The American Sex Revolution* (Boston: Porter Sargeant, 1956).

merit of economic and political systems by measuring their effects on this universal family.

Chapter 1 examines the unwritten social constitution of late-eighteenth-century America, rooted in the household economy, and traces the deliberate legal steps later taken to weaken the autonomous family. Chapter 2 looks to the great family wage experiment, during which American activists sought to salvage a cooperative home life in an industrial environment through massive cultural and legal manipulations of the labor market. The text traces the steady triumph of this concept in the Anglo-American world generally, and in the United States particularly, from 1840 to 1940 and then analyzes the dismantling of the family wage economy in the five decades that followed. Chapter 3 examines an alternate American strategy to preserve family life in the industrial age through the special environment of the suburb. Chapter 4 explores the power of religion to stimulate family behaviors that defy negative economic incentives, with a special focus on the successes and failures of the twentieth-century American faiths. Chapter 5 examines the attempted use of American nationalism as a substitute faith bonded to a socialist sense of solidarity, with the "Cold War" military family as the experimental model. Chapter 6 critically examines the most direct American effort to rebuild the severed bond between home and work: the crafting of the "profession" of home economics. The volume concludes with thoughts on current and future prospects for finding harmony between work and home in the lives of Americans.

One

The American
Constitutional Arrangement

The Constitution of the United States departs from a pattern
found among other written constitutions in the Western world:
it gives no attention to the institutions of marriage and family.
The constitution of the Fifth French Republic (1958 to present),
for example, makes lofty promises about defending the interests
of the family, as does the Basic Law of the Federal Republic
of Germany (1949 to present), as did the constitution of the
Weimar Republic (1919–33) before it. But marriage and family are not mentioned in the U.S. Constitution. Indeed, the
original document is even fairly clear of masculine language;
at times, it reads as though it were edited by the staff at the
old *Ms.* magazine. That awkward word *person* is used whenever
the generic word *man* would have sufficed, and the Founders
dutifully avoided any family-oriented language, such as "head
of household", to define those holding the franchise. Rather,
such decisions were left to the states.

In part, family issues are avoided in the U.S. Constitution,
because they were irrelevant: the document was a compact between thirteen sovereign states and was designed to solve a
given set of political and economic problems that had surfaced
under the Articles of Confederation; the status of the family
was not among these problems. More broadly, though, the
family was deeply embodied in the unwritten constitution of
the new United States, in the social views that the Founders
held. Indeed, their work rested on assumptions about the social order that must underlie a free republic, assumptions about
the sort of people they were dealing with and about the way
that citizens would live. In all the celebrating that marked the

bicentennial of the U.S. Constitution, recognition of this un-written constitution was largely absent.

Accordingly, it is profitable to consider the social order—the family system—that the Founders assumed would exist as the foundation of their enterprise. To do so, it is necessary to give particular emphasis to the importance they attached to the family economy or the home economy. It is also essential to examine the process through which American politicians dismantled large areas of this family economy: in the nineteenth century through both piece-meal responses to industrialization and a peculiar statist ideology, and in the twentieth century through the sys-tematic surrender of the U.S. Constitution's Tenth Amendment to the waxing power of the Fourteenth Amendment.

The social history of the constitutional period has been domi-nated by the Whiggish, or liberal, interpretation, which gives emphasis to American exceptionalism, the American difference. In his 1960 book *Education in the Forming of American Society,* Bernard Bailyn offered the classic argument, saying that the New World environment, alive with prospects of abundance and expansion, promoted the rise of a unique individualism. From the earliest settlements, "the ancient structure of family life", shaped by strong networks of kin and community, eroded in America, and the family retreated towards its marital "nuclear" core of man and woman. Meanwhile, the instability of the fron-tier situation promoted frequent migration. Out of this, con-cludes Bailyn, the modern American emerged, marked by a "sense of separateness" and a heightened individuality, that stood in sharp contrast to the kin-oriented peoples of old Europe. [1]

Variations on this argument also appear. In his detailed 1960 study of the frontier town of Kent, Connecticut, historian Charles Grant found a colonial population of proto-entrepre-neurs, with little sense of community or family loyalty. This

---

[1] Bernard Bailyn, *Education in the Forming of American Society: Needs and Op-portunities for Study* (Chapel Hill: University of North Carolina Press, 1960), 15–36.

was "a population raised on an economic tradition of land speculation and individualistic venturing", he reports, and they refused to make sacrifices for any cause other than themselves. As Grant puts it, "One sees in certain of the Kent settlers not so much the contented yeoman, . . . but perhaps the embryo John D. Rockefeller."[2] More recently, Jay Fliegelman's *Prodigals and Pilgrims* uses literary sources to document what he calls "the American revolution against patriarchal authority", arguing that our Founders translated their rebellion against parent country and patriarchal king to their private lives and so crafted a social revolution against the bonds of the traditional family.[3]

The central problem with this interpretation is its deterministic thrust: the suggestion that American history has been a process of evolution toward individualistic liberalism. As the engine of history ground along, all else fell aside.

A new kind of social history has emerged over the last twenty-five years that challenges this view of the revolutionary and constitutional periods and gives a very different understanding of the place of the family in this critical phase of the nation's past. Borrowing research questions and techniques from the French *Annales* school of historiography, these historians have offered a much richer, and decidedly different, portrait of America in the 1770s and 1780s. Instead of a nation of individualistic entrepreneurs and speculators, they see a land characterized by age stratification and patriarchal power, by strong kin connections and ethnic and religious communities, and by a household mode of production bonded to subsistence agriculture—in short, an America much closer to the hierarchical family systems of Europe than previously supposed.

This social system dominant in the late eighteenth century can be defined by five qualities:

[2] Charles S. Grant, *Democracy in the Connecticut Frontier Town of Kent* (New York: Norton, 1961), 53–54, 170–71.

[3] Jay Fliegelman, *Prodigals and Pilgrims: The American Revolution Against Patriarchal Authority, 1750–1800* (Cambridge, England: Cambridge University Press, 1982), 5–6, 263–67.

1. *The primacy of the family economy.* A few joint stock companies aside, most Americans in the late eighteenth century organized their economic lives around the family in the home. They arranged their labor along family lines rather than through a wage system. Most productive activities—from furniture construction and candle making through the raising and preparation of food—were family based. As the family gave symbolic and emotional meaning to subsistence activities, its own essence was shaped by the home-based character of production. Indeed, "family" and "economy" formed a rough unity, and family relations were conditioned by economic questions of property and labor. This family economy involved a complex web of obligations: parents enjoyed legal possession of property—as freeholders, tenants, or sharecroppers—and considered their own children as both dependents and workers through the culturally set age of majority. These adults were dependent on their children for economic support in old age and focused great attention on the terms and timing of the transfer of economic resources to the succeeding generation.[4]

In this home-centered economy, men and women performed quite different, although complementary, tasks, all of which were necessary for the survival of the family unit. Largely self-sufficient households, drawing supplemental help from a local exchange network of neighbors and kin, remained the focus of the lives of the vast majority of Americans well into the nineteenth century.[5]

[4] James A. Henretta, "Families and Farms: Mentality in Pre-Industrial America," *William and Mary Quarterly* 35 (Jan. 1978): 20–21.

[5] Joan R. Gunderson and Gwen Victor Gampel, "Married Women's Legal Status in Eighteenth-Century New York and Virginia", *William and Mary Quarterly* 39 (Jan. 1982): 127–29; Daniel Blake Smith, "The Study of the Family in Early America: Trends, Problems, and Prospects", *William and Mary Quarterly* (Jan. 1982): 15, 24; and Christopher Clark, "Household Economy, Market Exchange and the Rise of Capitalism in the Connecticut Valley, 1800–1860", *Journal of Social History* 13 (1979): 169–90.

The great diversity and productive capacity of these "family factories" are described in Rolla Milton Tryon, *Household Manufactures in the United States, 1640–1860* (Chicago: University of Chicago Press, 1917), particularly 188–241.

2. *The continued power of kinship and ethnic and religious communities.* New studies focused on towns and counties show the influence of religion over many aspects of daily life.[6] One paper studying York County, Pennsylvania, for example, reveals the varying life patterns of Ulster Presbyterians, German Lutherans, and English Quakers within the same small region. Differences in economic and inheritance patterns between the communities are contrasted with the persistence of those patterns over many generations.[7] Ethnic groups also formed closed economic communities: every name in the 1775 account book of shoemaker-butcher Henry King of Second River, New Jersey, was of Dutch origin; similarly, the main business connections of the Jewish, Quaker, and German merchants in Lancaster, Pennsylvania, were, without exception, with their respective coreligionists in Philadelphia.[8]

3. *The central focus on land.* The founding generation shared one overriding concern: land, particularly the preservation of the family freehold into the future. In his study of Quaker farmers in the Delaware Valley, Barry Levy found a population committed to the creation of families and the rearing of children as "tender plants growing in the Truth". The soil was their primary attachment, not as a speculative venture, but as the necessary foundation for a godly home. As these families acquired larger estates, the motivation was a "child-centered use of land". Indeed, the family served as a kind of revolving

[6] See John Demos, *A Little Commonwealth: Family Life in Plymouth Colony* (New York: Oxford University Press, 1970), 77–78.

[7] Daniel Snydacker, "Kinship and Community in Rural Pennsylvania", *Journal of Interdisciplinary History* 13 (Summer 1982): 41–61.

[8] Dennis P. Ryan, "Six Towns: Continuity and Change in Revolutionary New Jersey, 1770–1792", doctoral dissertation (New York: New York University, 1974), 57–71; and Jerome H. Wood, Jr., "Conestoga Crossroads: The Rise of Lancaster, Pennsylvania, 1730–1789", doctoral dissertation (Providence, RI: Brown University, 1969), 114–31.

fund, shifting land resources between generations over the life cycle.[9]

Looking at Andover, Massachusetts, Philip Greven, Jr., describes "the consuming concern" of fathers to see that their sons were settled on the land. Daniel Snydacker describes farms and families in late colonial America as "two halves of a corporate whole".[10] James Henretta emphasizes the central goal of the American population as the preservation of an agricultural society of yeoman freeholding families. Such farms, moreover, were not capitalist enterprises but were devoted to subsistence agriculture. Regional studies of the 1790s have shown that only 15 to 25 percent of farms produced sufficient surplus to engage in market transactions. Due to lack of markets and transportation networks, as well as to cultural preferences, the large majority of farms produced enough to feed the resident family and a little for barter with neighbors and kin in a noncash system of local exchange based on crude "just price" theories. In the middle and northern colonies, hired farm labor was rare: the account books of these families indicate that they invariably chose the security of diversified production rather than carrying the risks of hiring nonfarm labor and producing for sale.

Economic gain, although important to Americans, was not the overriding concern: it was subordinate to the long-run security, through land, of the family unit. Toward this end, the central goal of fathers was to provide for their children farms that were viable economic units. Even widow's rights—notably the customary "widow's third"—were subordinated to the protection of the estate. Property, in effect, was "communal" within the family, the aim being preservation of the land for posterity.[11]

[9] Barry Levy, "'Tender Plants': Quaker Farmers and Children in the Delaware Valley, 1681–1735", *Journal of Family History* 3 (Summer 1978): 116–29.

[10] Philip J. Greven, Jr., *Four Generations: Population, Land, and Family in Colonial Andover, Massachusetts* (Ithaca, NY: Cornell University Press, 1970), 251; and Snydacker, "Kinship and Community", 44.

[11] Henretta, "Families and Farms," 9, 12–15, 18–19, 28–29.

4. *The abundance of children.* In its reproductive patterns, the new United States was the equivalent of a modern Third World country — a demographic hot house, swarming with children. In 1790, one-half of the population was age 15 or younger, a phenomenon seen today only in places such as Kenya. One reliable estimate has a U.S. total fertility rate (TFR) in 1800 of 7.0, meaning roughly that the average woman of that generation bore seven children (by way of comparison, the current TFR is about 1.9). Recent studies suggest that fertility fell in the North American colonies between 1700 and 1725, partly in response to wars in Europe and partly due to constraints on new settlement. Yet between 1725 and 1800, fertility climbed again to historic high levels. A new fertility decline, although evident in some scattered groups shortly after 1775, did not occur on a widespread basis until well into the nineteenth century.[12]

In part, this remarkable fecundity reflected an unusual child centeredness. Seventeenth-century Quaker immigrants left England and settled in rural Pennsylvania, hoping that "it might be a good place to train up children amongst sober people and to prevent the corruption of them here by the loose behavior of youths and the bad example of too many of riper years."[13]

Children in America, though, were more than the accidental product of the sexual act or precious bundles to care for and nurture. They were also economic assets to their parents and extended families, new laborers for the family enterprise and sources of security for the care of the old. No less an ob-

---

[12] Daniel Scott Smith, "The Demographic History of Colonial New England", *Journal of Economic History* 32 (1972): 165, 179–82; Ansley J. Coale and Melvin Zelnick, *New Estimates of Fertility and Population in the United States* (Princeton, NJ: Princeton University Press, 1963); Maris Vinovskis, *Fertility in Massachusetts from the Revolution to the Civil War* (New York: Academic Press, 1981); and Robert V. Wells, "Family Size and Fertility Control in Eighteenth-Century America: A Study of Quaker Families", *Population Studies* 25 (Mar. 1971): 73–82.

[13] Quoted in Levy, "Tender Plants", 117.

server than Adam Smith, in his *Wealth of Nations* published in 1776, remarked that the rapid economic growth in England's American colonies both reflected and rested on the abundance of children: "Labor [in North America] is . . . so well rewarded that a numerous family of children, instead of being a burden, is a source of opulence and prosperity to the parents. The value of children is the greatest of all encouragements to marriage. We cannot, therefore, wonder that the people in North America should generally marry very young."[14]

These perceptions, moreover, were not illusions. Recent studies of both colonial Deerfield, Massachusetts, and contemporary Egypt confirm the point: in agricultural societies without the apparatus of a welfare state, children deliver tangible economic assets over the parents' life cycle, in terms of both wealth accumulation and security in old age.[15]

5. *The power of intergenerational bonds.* Late eighteenth-century America was age stratified, with older men using their control of financial resources — above all, land — to secure and maintain status and power. Age, not class, appears to have been the principal agent of social control. The young were relatively powerless; the old used elaborate methods of gifts and bequests to bind their children to them. Widows usually remained dependent on their children through a complex mix of inheritance and customary services in kind. As historian James Henretta has put it, parents raised children to "succeed them", not merely to "succeed". Through this orientation, the agricultural family remained a lineal one. Although each generation lived in separate households, the nature of production and methods of inheritance bound these nuclear units through many ties. Duties

[14] Adam Smith, *An Inquiry into the Nature and Causes of the Wealth of Nations,* ed. C. J. Bullock (New York: Collier & Son, 1903), 74–75.

[15] Nancy R. Folbre, "The Wealth of Patriarchs: Deerfield, Massachusetts, 1760–1840", *Journal of Interdisciplinary History* 16 (Autumn 1985): 217–19; and Eva Mueller, "The Economic Value of Children in Peasant Agriculture", in *Population and Development: The Search for Selective Interventions,* ed. Ronald G. Ridker (Baltimore, MD: Johns Hopkins University Press, 1976), 146.

and rights criss-crossed the generations. As Henretta concluded: "The line was more important than the individual; the patrimony was to be conserved for lineal reasons."[16]

These five qualities—the primacy of the family economy, the continued power of kinship and community, the central focus on land, the abundance of children, and the power of intergenerational bonds—defined the social order of America in the years before, during, and immediately after the Revolution and the drafting of the Constitution. Having particular strength in the agrarian societies of the North and upland South, the lineal family stood at the center of American economic and social existence. Judging from the evidence of diaries, letters, and wills, it is clear that most men, women, and children viewed their world through this prism of family commitments, and the same evidence suggests that family concerns shaped the assumptions with which the Constitution's writers worked. They understood the family unit as setting constraints on the individual, as forcing a balance between a person's quest for power and goods and the needs of the community and posterity. This family-centered world put limits around private ambition, the entrepreneurial spirit, and even religious membership. The Founders assumed that most American eyes would be turned toward home, which would provide an ordered society within a regime of liberty. And they also assumed that the home must have an economic base: that it could not survive as the center of moral power if it was stripped of its economic power and independence.[17]

Defense of this social order, this society of households, lay

[16] Henretta, "Families and Farms", 30, 26. See also Greven, *Four Generations,* 221, 253–58; and "Widowhood in Eighteenth Century Massachusetts: A Problem in the History of the Family", *Perspectives in American History,* Vol. 8, ed. Donald Fleming and Bernard Bailyn (Cambridge, MA: Harvard University Press, 1974), 83–119.

[17] John E. Crowley, "The Importance of Kinship: Testamentary Evidence from South Carolina", *Journal of Interdisciplinary History* 16 (1986): 576–77; and Henretta, "Families and Farms", 32.

with the states and the people. The U.S. Constitution presumed a nation of families and ultimately relied on the spirit behind the Bill of Rights—specifically, the Ninth and Tenth Amendments, which reserved the rights of the people and the power of the states—as the primary bulwark against social experimentation. Unfortunately, these did not prove to be enough.

The American family system faced new challenges in the early nineteenth century, particularly in New England. The expansion of markets and early industry made the payment of wages more common, leaving sons less dependent on fathers, fathers less dependent on sons, and families less bound to home production. The growing influence of land speculators, bankers, and mortgage companies also disturbed assumptions about land and family that together had woven the social order.[18]

The factory posed the greatest challenge to the family system. For two generations, available technology and cultural pressures kept industry largely within the home. Through the 1830s, the family factory—involving production for market sale and the application of the division of labor—remained dominant. This system of home work, or household manufacture, drew female labor into the market economy without dislocating the family as the center of economic life or seriously disrupting gender roles. This, in turn, preserved the reciprocal economic bonds between parents and children.[19]

However, in the white South, the prevailing family system of the United States remained strong, with no significant challenge through the whole period up to the Civil War. In this region, the family served as the main source of personal security, advancement, and assistance. Definitions of selfhood sprang from one's family ties; personal ambition and glory rested on survival of the family name and patrimony and their promise and heritage for the unborn. The individual sought to make

[18] Folbre, "Wealth of Patriarchs", 204–5.

[19] Tryon, *Household Manufactures,* 243–76; and Paul G. Faler, "Workingmen, Mechanics and Social Change: Lynn, Massachusetts, 1800–1860", doctoral dissertation (Madison: University of Wisconsin, 1971).

his mark through blood ties, not through the accumulation of goods or power. As John C. Calhoun once explained, the southern states were a collection of communities, not of individuals. The family, with the father and husband at its head, was the agency for setting daily routine, defining social conventions and deviance, and setting the lines of social order. Believing that power belonged in the home, southerners battled the encroachments of other institutions — governmental bureaucracies, common schools, and even national church bodies — that threatened family order. By 1860, for example, the average child in the mid-Atlantic states spent 157 days in school; in the South, only 80 days, a fact reflecting the common view that the family, not the school, should be the bearer of ideals to the young, particularly through oral tradition and example.

Even the peculiar southern custom of marriage between cousins was driven by the desire to preserve and, if possible, extend the family patrimony and to ensure personal security. This family system was also pronatalist, or probirth, by social convention. A family with numerous children brought honor to the parents. At the same time, antebellum southerners feared becoming dependent on the state government. In short, as historian Bertram Wyatt-Brown concludes, "What nineteenth-century whites [in the South] claimed to be, they actually were — a people devoted on the whole to founding families, sometimes creating princely lines by their standards, and preserving elemental distinctions of blood, race, and gender."[20]

Since the 1840s, American social history could be written as the steady dismantling of this home-centered economy and the consequent decay of the foundations of liberty. Pressures brought by industrialization's disruption of the home-labor bond were aggravated by a statist ideology that cast the family as historically doomed.

[20] Bertram Wyatt-Brown, "The Ideal Typology and Antebellum Southern History: A Testing of a New Approach", *Societas* 5 (Winter 1975): 29; also George Fitzhugh, *Sociology for the South, or the Failure of Free Society* (Richmond, VA: A. Morris, 1854).

The first direct assault on family autonomy grew out of the reform school movement during the 1830s. This movement, centered in the early years in New York and Pennsylvania, advocated removing poor and so-called neglected or delinquent children from parents and placing them in institutions to "prevent" them from entering a life of crime. In 1839, the Pennsylvania Supreme Court declared such actions constitutional. Twisting an ancient concept of English chancery law designed to protect the estates of orphaned minors, the court established a new doctrine in American law: *parens patriae,* literally "the parenthood of the state." Justifying the termination of parental rights, the justices stated: "May not the natural parents, when unequal to the task of education or unworthy of it, be supplanted by the *parens patriae,* or common guardianship of the community?"[21] This elevation of the state over the family rapidly expanded into a sweeping usurpation of American liberties. As the Illinois Supreme Court ruled in 1882:

> It is the unquestioned right and imperative duty of every enlightened government, in its character of *parens patriae,* to protect and provide for the comfort and well-being of such of its citizens as, by reason of infancy, defective understanding, or other misfortune or infirmity, are unable to take care of themselves. The performance of this duty is justly regarded as one of the most important of governmental functions, and all constitutional limitations must be so understood and construed so as not to interfere with its proper and legitimate exercise.[22]

Through logic of this sort, the family was stripped of elemental legal protection.

The same spirit animated the public school movement and the compulsory education laws that gave this movement power. Horace Mann and his fellow common-school enthusiasts sought to use state education to immerse the new Irish Catholic immigrants in Massachusetts in a special mix of religious Unitarianism

[21] *Ex Parte Crouse,* 4 Wharton, Pa. 9 (1838).
[22] *County of McLean* v. *Humphreys,* 104, Ill. 383 (1882).

and political liberalism. At a deeper level, the school reforms cut into the fabric of the family economy, stripping children in large part of their economic value and removing parents from control of their offsprings' upbringing.[23]

The proponents of state schooling were rarely reticent about their motives. As one South Carolina school inspector, in arguing for a compulsory attendance law, explained in 1912: "The schools exist primarily for the benefit of the State rather than for the benefit of the individual. The State seeks to make every citizen intelligent and serviceable." He mocked concern about "the sacred rights and personal privileges" of parents who kept their children at home:

> The State has the right to carry the lawbreaking child to the reformatory or to jail to protect society. Has not the State as much right to carry the child to the school . . . to train him to benefit society? Those who deny the right of the State to compel the parent to send his child to school are too frequently the offending parents themselves, sentimental theorists or vacillating politicians.[24]

Court decisions on the constitutionality of compulsory attendance laws regarded parental rights as secondary to both the "welfare of the minor" and the interests of the state. According to the Indiana Supreme Court in a 1901 decision, the natural rights of a parent to the custody and control of his infant child were subordinate to the power of the government. In this vein, the school attendance law was not only constitutional, but also "necessary" to the very purposes of the Indiana Constitution itself.[25] A related decision in Pennsylvania argued that the public had "a paramount interest" in the virtue and knowledge of its members and that, "of strict right", the business of education belonged to the state. Accordingly, the educa-

[23] Folbre, "Wealth of Patriarchs", 213.
[24] W. H. Hand, "Need for Compulsory Education in the South", *Child Labor Bulletin* 1 (June 1912): 79.
[25] *State* v. *Bailey,* 157 Ind. 324 (1901).

tional function of the family not only could be, but should be stripped away. Significantly, the Pennsylvania justices referred with admiration to recent U.S. Supreme Court interpretations of the Fourteenth Amendment, particularly the new view of law as "a progressive science" that must always alter a settled principle with an expansive interpretation that would meet "advancing and changing conditions".[26]

Indeed, the twentieth century bore witness to the progressive sacrifice of the U.S. Constitution's Tenth Amendment, which declares that powers not specifically granted the federal government are reserved to the states, to both the growing sweep of the Fourteenth Amendment and to the burgeoning welfare state. The press for a federal child labor law, for example, rested again on the conscious repudiation of states' rights, parental rights, and the family economy. Parents' control over the training and future of their children, advocates said, must be subordinated to the higher interests and higher wisdom of the central state. Individual states allowing parents flexibility, particularly offenders in the South, would have to be brought into line.[27]

The crafting of the old age benefits portion of the Social Security system also aimed at dismantling another aspect of the home economy: intergenerational security. In its 1935 report to the President, the Committee on Economic Security noted that "children, friends, and relatives have borne and still carry the major costs of supporting the aged." But the committee used the circumstances of "the present depression" to push for a state system that would, over time, replace family insurance with social insurance.[28]

[26] *Commonwealth* v. *Edsall,* 13 Pa. D.R. 509 (1903). See also John Frederick Bender, *The Functions of Courts in Enforcing School Attendance Laws* (New York: Teachers College Press, 1927), 10–19.

[27] Katharine DuPre Lumpkin and Dorothy Wolff Douglas, *Child Workers in America* (New York: Robert M. McBride, 1937), 86, 94–96, 236–37.

[28] *Report to the President of the Committee on Economic Security* (Washington, DC: U.S. Government Printing Office, 1935), 23–25.

Legal challenges to the Social Security system focused on the Tenth Amendment and the charge that the new laws violated rights reserved to the states. The U.S. Supreme Court, though, rejected the argument, using the economic crisis to sweep aside the states' rights complaint. More importantly, the court also referred to that unfounded legal concept, the parenthood of the state, as justification for the new welfare mentality: "The *parens patriae* has many reasons — fiscal and economic as well as social and moral — for planning to mitigate disasters that bring these burdens in their train."[29]

Federal family welfare laws have also subverted the economic integrity of the family. Although the spirit had been growing for decades, Herbert Hoover's 1930 White House Conference on Child Health and Protection marked the triumph of a new conception of the state's child. The 1909 White House conference, enthusiasts noted, had mainly aimed at deinstitutionalizing orphans and delinquent children, and the 1919 conference had focused on child labor. But with the 1930 assembly, they noted cheerily: "The [state's] emphasis swung very definitely from dependent and handicapped children . . . to all children, of the whole family of the nation, wherever they lived and whatever their situation." Indeed, one semi-official product of the conference described a new entity: "Uncle Sam's Child", a product "who belongs to the community almost as much as to the family", a "new racial experiment", and a citizen of "a world predestinedly moving toward unity". The same volume attacked the rural home and the rural family — legacies of the old vision — as psychologically inadequate, while praising public schools as "a community power with more potential influence for orienting the child to his environment than any other".[30]

This new spirit further undermined the economic founda-

---

[29] *Steward Machine Co.* v. *Davis,* 301 U.S. 548 (1937). See also Robert Stevens, ed., *Statutory History of the United States: Income Security* (New York: Chelsea House, 1970), 188–214.

[30] Katharine Glover and Evelyn Dewey, *Children of the New Day* (New York: D. Appleton-Century, 1934), 4–12, 183, 195, 200.

tions of family life. At first, federal welfare programs seemed traditionalist in intent. Indeed, the 1935 report of Roosevelt's Committee on Economic Security defended the proposed Aid to Dependent Children program as an affirmation of stay-at-home motherhood: "[These measures] are designed to release from the wage-earning role the person whose natural function is to give her children the physical and affectionate guardianship necessary not only to keep them from falling into social misfortune, but more affirmatively to rear them into citizens capable of contributing to society."[31] But, in fact, this new measure merely represented another step in dissolving the natural family economy by separating women from the need for a bond to men when raising children. Indeed, by the latter 1970s, the system was fully skewed toward support of the modern "mother-state-child" family, to the exclusion of fathers. The state had become the breadwinner. Recently, economists Lowell Gallaway and Richard Vedder calculated that until a child reached age 12, welfare benefits actually exceeded the cost of raising a child; by the time the child reached age 17, benefits exceeded costs by $3,000.[32] At the same time, the U.S. Supreme Court struck down attempts to condition public assistance on "marriage" or "family" status, arguing that the denial of benefits to persons in new or novel life-styles violated the "equal protection" standards of the Fourteenth Amendment.[33]

The U.S. Supreme Court's recent rulings on the meaning of marriage have followed a similar course, undermining the family economy. Back in 1888, the court described marriage as "something more than a mere contract. . . . It is an institution, in the maintenance of which in its purity the public is deeply

[31] *Report to the President*, 36.

[32] Lowell Gallaway and Richard Vedder, *Poverty, Income Distribution, the Family and Public Policy* (Washington, DC: Joint Economic Committee, U.S. Congress, 1986), 61–62.

[33] *New Jersey Welfare Rights Organization* v. *Cahill*, 411 U.S. 619 (1973); and *King* v. *Smith*, 392 U.S. 309 (1968).

interested, for it is the foundation of the family of society."[34] As late as 1965, the court recognized in *Griswold* v. *Connecticut* that "marriage is a coming together for better or worse, hopefully enduring, and intimate to the degree of being sacred."[35] But in 1972, a mere seven years later, the court used the logic of the Fourteenth Amendment to strip marriage of most meaning, arguing that "the marital couple is not an independent entity with a heart and mind of its own, but an association of two individuals each with a separate intellectual and emotional make up." Accordingly, marriage could no longer have a preferred status.[36]

The federal income tax has also been altered in recent decades in an effort to tax residual home production. The 1972 expansion of the income tax deduction granted to parents using day care, the substitution in 1976 of the Child Care Tax Credit, and the special tax credit given to two-income married couples in 1981 were all designed, at the expert level, as a way of indirectly taxing the services of the mother at home — namely, her labor in areas such as child care and food preparation. For the first time, the Internal Revenue Service successfully invaded hearth and home and imposed an indirect tax on the intimate exchanges within the private family economy.[37]

In sum, assumptions about the family basis of social order and economic exchange have been subverted, while the prevailing interpretation of the Fourteenth Amendment has undermined the ability of the Tenth Amendment to defend states and their inhabitants against intrusions by the national government.

If the Founders of this nation were correct, if this unwritten

[34] *Maynard* v. *Hill,* 125 U.S. 190, 210–11 (1888).

[35] *Griswold* v. *Connecticut,* 381 U.S. 486 (1965).

[36] *Eisenstadt* v. *Baird,* 495 U.S. 438, 453 (1972). On the general trend in recent court decisions against marriage, see Carl Anderson, "The Supreme Court and the Economics of the Family", *The Family in America* 1 (Oct. 1987): 1–8.

[37] See Allan Carlson, "A Pro-Family Income Tax", *The Public Interest* 94 (Winter 1989): 69–76.

constitution was important to healthy social order, then recent changes in law should have contributed to rising measures of social disarray. Statistical measures suggest that this has occurred. The number of annual divorces in the United States rose steadily between 1890 and 1940, stabilized for several decades, and then tripled between 1960 and 1981, rising to 1,213,000. Over the same twenty-one-year period, the number of children annually affected by divorce more than doubled. With the economic logic of marriage under siege, the rate of first marriage declined by 30 percent after 1960; among women ages 20 through 24, the fall was an astonishing 60 percent. With children stripped of economic value, the birthrate fell sharply after 1890, recovered some ground between 1940 and 1960, and then plunged from 118 (births per 1,000 women, ages 15 through 44) in 1960 to only 65 in 1978. All of this decline occurred among married-couple families. Indeed, with illegitimate births drawing extensive state subsidy, their number quadrupled, from 224,000 in 1960 to over 1,000,000 in 1989.

Moreover, there is compelling evidence that these dramatic changes in American social life have been linked, in turn, to a rise in juvenile crime, a sharp increase in the incidence of drug abuse, the decay in the educational performance of youth, a sharp rise in youth suicide, and (in part) soaring levels of health care costs.[38] Stripped of its economic, educational, and security functions, the institution of the family lay prostrate before the looming power of its ancient rival, the state.

---

[38] See Allan Carlson, *Family Questions: Reflections on the American Social Crisis* (New Brunswick, NJ: Transaction Books, 1988), 257–72; Bryce Christensen, "The Costly Retreat from Marriage", *The Public Interest* 91 (Spring 1988): 59–66; and Allan Carlson and Bryce Christensen, "Educational Content within 'The Bourgeois Family'", paper prepared for the conference on "Education and Family", Office for Educational Research, U.S. Department of Education, June 1988.

Two

The Family Wage Experiment

Jack was sitting before the hearth fire, darning his working wife's sock. A tear lay in his eye. "No," the wretched man said in a thick Yorkshire accent, "there is plenty of Wark for Wemen and Bairns [children] in this quarter but very Little for men—thou may as well go try to finde a hondred pounds, as go to find wark abouts heare—but I hed not ment neather thee nor eney one Els to have seen me manding t'wife's stockings, for its a poar job."

The bloke wiped away the tear. "I do not [k]now what is to become of us," he whimpered, "for she as been't'man now for a Long time, and me t'woman—it is hard wark." When he had married, Jack said, he held a fine job and the couple "gat on very well—we got a good firnished Home. . . . I could wark for us boath." But now "t'world is turned up side down. Mary has to turn out to wark and I have to stop at home to mind Bairns—and to Wash and Clean—Bake and mend." At that point, Jack lost control and wept violently, declaring over and again his wish that he had never been born.[1]

This peculiar story, borrowed from Friedrich Engels' communist classic, *The Condition of the Working Class in England,* reflects both the considerable passions and the odd ideological alignments to be found in mid-nineteenth-century Anglo-American debates on the fate of the family. Beneath them, though, lay the central social problem. The steady industrialization of Western economies after 1750 placed great stress on the prevailing social order resting on rural life and a home-centered economy. Among the most urgent questions raised

---

[1] Friedrich Engels, *The Condition of the Working Class in England,* trans. W. O. Henderson and W. H. Chaloner (New York: Macmillan, 1958), 162-63.

was how to structure family life and gender roles within a competitive labor market: the issue of the family wage.

The emergence of market capitalism threw the settled agrarian world into disarray. As Karl Marx phrased it, machinery and a new specialization of labor squeezed itself into one process after another, making way for constant change. The workplace and the home lost the unity they enjoyed under the farming and guild systems. Moreover, the natural, complementary roles of men and women in marriage gave way to a potential new competition, with husband and wife now able to bid against each other in the sale of their labor to a third party. Children, too, no longer found a natural economic niche in a home-based family enterprise. Instead, they also became potential workers in the factories, competitors against their parents for the same work.

As guild-imposed restraints on production, price, and income crumbled, another problem gained attention: the unequal social burdens borne by those workers with children, compared to those without. Unlike the farm economy, a competitive wage market took no direct account of family size. All other things being equal, a bachelor and a man with five small children would receive the same wage for a day's work, yet their burdens were vastly different. If children could be seen simply as a commodity, a consumption choice, there was no difficulty. But if they bore some intrinsic worth greater than that of beasts or goods, the imbalance between the child-rich and the childless demanded attention.

From Adam Smith in the late eighteenth century to Alfred Marshall in the late nineteenth century, the early political economists wrestled with these family questions and their relation to demographic trends considered vital to long-term prosperity. When turning to families and wages, Smith developed two primary themes. On the one hand, he saw children in a progressive economy as a continued source of wealth, with the labor of each child, before it left the home, "computed to be worth a hundred pounds clear gain" to parents. On the other

hand, he presumed that adult labor would be primarily responsible for family support: "[I]n order to bring up a family," he
wrote, "the labor of the husband and wife together must, even
in the lowest species of common labor, be able to earn something more than what is precisely necessary for their own maintenance."

In drawing these themes together, Smith borrowed a concept from the Physiocrats: the natural wage, where the price
of labor would correspond to the value of the product; in this
case, to the cost of subsistence for the laborer and his family.
Moving beyond direct observation and into psychology and
a kind of metaphysics, Smith argued that "parental tenderness"
was innate to the human species and naturally much stronger
than even filial piety, since the reproduction and survival of
the species depended on it. Hence, he believed that sentiments
of "common humanity" would ensure delivery of a natural
wage commensurate with natural family duties. Beyond that
natural minimum wage, a progressive, expanding economy
would stimulate larger families, for "the demand for men, like
that for any other commodity, necessarily regulates the production of men." Smith was not unmindful of potential problems
in the distribution of wealth in a growing economy, including
those involving family support. But he believed that the focus
should be on production and that the consequent expansion
in wealth would spread over time to all. Attempts by government to interfere in the distribution of income would only
retard growth, reduce potential wealth, and forestall a natural
family wage.[2]

Writing in 1799, Thomas Robert Malthus said that such a
progressive economy, favorable to family life and procreation,
was impossible. The law of population, he reasoned, would
translate any real increase in wages into more births, which

[2] Smith, *Inquiry into . . . the Wealth of Nations,* 71–75, 84; and Adam Smith,
The Theory of Moral Sentiments (New Rochelle, NY: Arlington House, 1969),
195, 321.

would drive family living standards, for a time, back below bare subsistence levels, resulting in misery and death. Only the moral check of delayed marriage, and consequent fewer children, could allow societies to break out of this vicious cycle. He railed, in particular, against the Speenhamland system, or the Poor Laws, which spread throughout England after 1796. Representing an early governmental attempt at reconciling wages and family burden, this plan advocated that parishes pay an allowance to day laborers, calculated according to their number of children. Malthus argued that these family allowances had "the fatal and unavoidable consequence of continually increasing" the number of the poor, and so depressing the condition of workers struggling to remain independent. He predicted that the Poor Laws would drive down real wages so as "to make the common wages of day labor insufficient to support a single child without parish support". At the same time, single persons found themselves penalized, whereas inappropriate early marriages were encouraged. He urged reform of the Poor Laws so as "not to depress the wages of labor below what is sufficient for the support of the average number of children that might be expected from each marriage". [3]

David Ricardo shared both Malthus' dislike of the Speenhamland system and Smith's faith in a natural, family-sustaining minimum wage. Rising real wages, he maintained, would require a high rate of capital accumulation, which could only come through "prudential checks" on family size. This, he believed, was possible. The broader problem, Ricardo said, was state interference, specifically the English Poor Laws and the child allowances that depressed real wages below a family-sustaining level. They must be repealed, he insisted: "Everything would go on well if we could rescue the lowest laborers with families from an habitual reliance on the rates." Respond-

[3] See T. R. Malthus, *A Letter to Samuel Whitbread on His Proposed Bill for the Amendment of the Poor Laws* (London: J. Johnson, St. Paul's Churchyard, 1807); reproduced in *The Pamphlets of Thomas Robert Malthus* (New York: Augustus M. Kelley, 1970), 37–41, 46.

ing to the grim Malthusian scenario, Ricardo wrote in 1821: "If men depended wholly on their own exertions for support, a state of society might and I think would exist, in which it could not be 'successfully shown that no laborer and very few artisans have a prospect of being able to maintain a family'". He had confidence that the unfettered wage market resting on common sense and humane sensibilities would produce a natural family wage, where "[a] man's wages should, and would on a really good system, be sufficient not only to maintain himself and family when he is in full work, but also to enable him to lay up a provision . . . for those extraordinary calls." Ricardo acknowledged that single men, without families, would reap "a surplus" from this development, yet he expected them to turn this into savings. To charges that single persons would spend the money in idle pleasures, Ricardo dissented. "Even if [the surplus for single men] were an evil, which I think it is not, it must be endured for the sake of the good which would accompany it."[4]

Supply and demand for labor, John Stuart Mill argued, was the sole regulator of wages. With Malthus, he agreed that under natural conditions, families would always reproduce down to bare subsistence. But if workers learned to control their reproduction and so restrict the labor pool, their conditions would improve. Mill shared Ricardo's abhorrence of the Poor Laws, which, he said, encouraged early marriage, the birth of additional children, a preference for the employment of the married over the unmarried, a decline in real wages, and long-term dependency. Give the poor a children's allowance, Mill said, and they toss out self-restraint. To charges of hard-heartedness, Mill replied that it was "a thousand times more hard-hearted to tell human beings that they may . . . call into existence swarms of creatures who are sure to be miserable,

[4] Letters, Ricardo to Trower, Jan. 26, 1818; and Ricardo to Place, Sept. 9, 1821; quoted in Samuel Hollander, *The Economics of David Ricardo* (Toronto and Buffalo: University of Toronto Press, 1979), 577, 581; see also 547–58, 555–59, 574–81.

and most likely to be depraved". He acknowledged that "[e]very-one has a right to live. . . . But no one has a right to bring creatures into life, to be supported by other people." Child allowances, he continued, were merely another minimum wage scheme that would reduce the number of jobs actually available and ultimately force the state to provide work for those left unemployed. The market, he insisted, must be allowed to function among both wages and men.

Yet this was true only to a degree. For alongside this defense of economic liberty (not to mention his famed affirmation of women's rights in *The Subjection of Women*), Mill called on women laborers to return home. He noted that the worst paid trades were those in which wives and children worked alongside male artisans, which drove down wages to levels where "the aggregate earnings of a family are lower than in almost any other kind of industry". Mill concluded: "It cannot . . . be considered desirable as a permanent element in the condition of a laboring class, that the mother of the family . . . should be under the necessity of working for subsistence, at least elsewhere than in their place of abode." Consistent with this, he said that the wages of single women "must be equal to their support, but need not be more than equal". At the same time, "the man's wages must be at least sufficient to support himself, a wife, and a number of children adequate to keep up the population, since if it were less, the population would not be kept up." Mill, in short, championed a family wage system built on differing remunerations for women and men, a purposeful inequality.[5]

The political economists of socialism denied that the capitalist system could ever deliver such a wage. In *The Condition of the Working Class in England,* Friedrich Engels argued that the introduction of machines and the capitalists' division of labor

[5] John Stuart Mill, *Principles of Political Economy, with Some of Their Applications to Social Philosophy,* 1871 ed. (New York: Augustus M. Kelley, 1961), 343–79, 399–401.

drove out skilled labor. Owners discovered that the machines could be run by women or children at a half or a third of the rates paid men. The latter would be dismissed or would accept "children's work at children's wages". As noted earlier, Engels devoted a remarkable four pages to an assault on the growing number of househusbands, where "the normal division of labor within the family" had been reversed. He described this state of affairs as "senseless and foolish", "shameful and degrading", a "mockery . . . of humanity and its aspirations". Continuing his focus on capitalism's impact on the family, Engels wrote: "It is inevitable that if a married woman works in a factory, family life is . . . destroyed and . . . its dissolution has the most demoralizing consequences both for parents and children." Children lacked parental care and were "left to run wild". Infant mortality rose. Husbands drifted into saloons. Breastfeeding became impossible. Indignant, Engels concluded that "a married woman cannot really be regarded as a mother if she is unable to spare the time to look after her child." Such mothers fostered "the universal decadence of family life among the workers".[6]

In *Capital,* Karl Marx used his observations of England to build on this argument. The pressures of competition, Marx said, drove the capitalist to find the least expensive workers he could. This translated into the "shameless", "unconscionable" exploitation of entire families and the degeneration of family bonds: "The wretched half-starved parents think of nothing but getting as much as possible out of their children. The latter . . . do not care a farthing . . . for their parents, and leave them." For Marx, though, these family-destroying developments were a central part of the historical transformation leading to the world revolution. It was only by drawing ever more family members into the labor force at ever shrinking real wages, he said, that capitalists could squeeze more "surplus value" out of human labor. Moreover, it was the growing

[6] Engels, *Condition of the Working Class,* 151–53, 159–64, 167–68, 182–83.

misery of the working family and its unnatural, distorted structure that would create conditions for the new order. As Marx
explained: "However terrible and disgusting the dissolution,
under the capitalist system, of the old family ties may appear,
nevertheless, modern industry, by assigning as it does an important part in the process of production, outside the domestic sphere, to women, to young persons, and to children of both
sexes, creates a new economic foundation for a higher form
of the family and of the relation between the sexes."[7]

In his summary of classical nineteenth-century economic
thought, Alfred Marshall essentially acknowledged the same
economic pressures that cut away at family bonds. Concerning child labor, he wrote that "[m]achinery has displaced many
men, but not many boys." Customary restrictions that had excluded children from numerous trades were also giving way.
Although some good was being done, Marshall acknowledged
that these changes "are doing harm in this, that they are en-
abling boys, and even girls, to set their parents at defiance and
start in life on their own account". Similarly, the wages of
women were rising fast relative to those of men, and more
women were attracted into the labor force. This, he said, was
a "great gain" as it helped "to develop their faculties". But it
was, too, an injury "in so far as it tempts them to neglect their
duty of building up a true home, and of investing their efforts
in the personal capital of their children's character and abilities". In line with this, Marshall described the "necessaries" of
a laborer's wage to include "sufficient freedom for his wife from
other work to enable her to perform properly her maternal and
her household duties".[8]

Smith, Ricardo, and Marx agreed on one point: the wage
market should be allowed to function freely. Smith and Ricardo

---

[7] Karl Marx, *Capital: A Critique of Political Economy,* ed. Frederick Engels,
trans. Samuel Moore and Edward Aveling (New York: Modern Library, 1906),
504–20.

[8] Alfred Marshall, *Principles of Economics,* 3rd ed. (London: Macmillan, 1985),
bk. 2, chap. 4; bk. 6, chap. 12.

were fairly confident that the results would be favorable: a
natural wage sufficient for family sustenance would result
through the interplay of market forces and innate human sentiments. Marx, for his part, was confident that the impact of
competitive wages on family life was a central contradiction
of capitalism, driving the engine of history toward revolution.

Most people, though, were unwilling to leave the question
to the play of economic forces. Over the following decades,
there emerged three different strategies for intentionally constructing a family wage economy. Although varying in their
degree of complexity, each of these strategies played a role in
blocking the free play of economic forces and so deferring an
answer to the question of whether Smith or Marx was right.

1. Defense of the Autonomous Home

Those who championed the home as an intentionally separate,
morally superior sphere of life appeared in the early decades
of the industrial revolution. In England in the 1790s, for example, the merchant-followers of religious reformer William
Wilberforce removed their families from the moral and environmental pollutions of London and resettled in Clapham,
south of the Thames. In constructing the first true suburb, the
"Clapham sect" viewed the village on the periphery, supplemented by the men's daily commute to the city, as the means
of reconciling commercial society with rural, family-centered
virtues. Their town represented a community of shared values,
including Christian duty, spontaneous family affection, and the
love and nurturing of children. With fathers and husbands at-
tending to economic matters, the home would serve as the
center of family worship and education.

The women of Clapham viewed their elevation of the moral
and religious life of the home as the basis for renewal of civilization. Although bound to domestic duties, they saw their work
as decidedly superior to the mean tasks of their husbands. A

typical figure was Marianne Thornton, wife of merchant Henry Thornton. A fervent Evangelical before her marriage at age 21, she turned her energies to the construction of a Christian family. The mother of nine children, she rejected the custom found among the old London elite of sending children to a wet nurse. Rather, she breastfed all of them herself and devoted her life to the religious training of the family. [9]

In America, the same orientation found a popular defense in the books and essays of Catharine Beecher. Vividly aware of the new economic world of individualism and competition, Beecher concluded that virtue, true religion, and family bonds could survive only if the home was radically separated from the world of commerce and paid work. Men, she reasoned, were irretrievably drawn into the world of "outdoor labor", and would so be excluded from many of "the comforts of a home". It fell to women to renounce competitive ways and to construct homes that were islands of antimodernity within the industrial sea. In what she called the "family state", the "father undergoes toil and self-denial to provide a home", whereas "the mother becomes a self-sacrificing laborer" to rear the children found within. Beecher believed that every woman should be trained to earn a livelihood, but that this should be put aside for the higher goal of creating a Christian home. "Thus the discipline of the family state is one of daily self-devotion of the stronger and wiser to elevate and support the weaker members." Women must transform homes into a combination of habitat, school, and church, where sharing and love might survive. "The family state", she concluded, "is the aptest illustration of the heavenly kingdom, and in it woman is its chief minister." [10]

[9] A good survey of life in Clapham is found in Robert Fishman, *Bourgeois Utopias: The Rise and Fall of Suburbia* (New York: Basic Books, 1987), 18–72.

[10] Catharine E. Beecher, *An Essay on the Education of Female Teachers* [1835], in *The Educated Woman in America,* ed. Barbara M. Cross (New York: Teachers College Press, 1965), 67–75; and Catharine Beecher and Harriet Beecher Stowe, *The American Woman's Home, or Principles of Domestic Science* (New York: J. B. Ford, 1869), chap. 1.

In short, the women of Clapham, Beecher, and their many cobelievers presumed that married women should voluntarily renounce their participation in the paid labor force: in effect, ignore the economic forces that craved their labor. Payment of a family wage to male heads-of-households was not explicitly part of their plan; but it was implicit in their assumptions. The father should be in the competitive work force, earning a wage sufficient to sustain a family; the mother should be in the home, building a small Christian commonwealth.

2. Constructing a Nongovernmental Family Wage

There were numerous attempts in this period to deliver a family wage to male heads-of-households, as a moral obligation free of state coercion. The thinking behind the voluntary family wage reached its fullest expression within the Roman Catholic tradition.

Prior theorizing by moral theologians on the doctrine of the "just price" formed the basis for Catholic thought on wages. Although Thomas Aquinas gave no direct attention to the wages of day laborers, probably because there were so few in his day, he did cherish the idea of a fair price independent of individual judgments, a price with "objective justness" that partook of divine justice and helped bring social harmony.

Moral theologians of the early modern era, including Molina (d. 1600), Lessius (d. 1623), Bonacina (d. 1631), and DeLugo (d. 1600), were the first to turn to consideration of moral obligations to the propertyless worker. They said, or implied, that he was owed a wage adequate to the sustenance of his own life and the lives of his dependents. In a thorough investigation of the course of moral theology on this issue in the 1750–1890 period, James Healy has shown that the overwhelming majority of Catholic writers on moral theology — from St. Alphonsus of Ligouri (d. 1787) to George Crolly (d. 1878) —

held opinions that logically demanded a family living wage as a matter of justice.[11]

During the mid-nineteenth century, new Catholic voices gave concrete attention to the condition of industrial workers and sought to carve out a Christian democracy, neither liberal nor socialist. Frederic Ozanam condemned both the vices of individualism and the antifamily attitudes spawned by socialism. He said that employers were under a moral obligation to pay laborers a wage adequate to their own proper living and the education of their children and also sufficient for retirement from work in their declining years. Bishop William Emanuel von Ketteler, the spiritual force behind the Christian labor union movement, said, "The power of money without religion is an evil, but the power of organized labor without religion is just as great an evil. Both lead to destruction." He urged organized Catholic workers to press for fair hours, the prohibition of child labor, the sharp limitation of female labor ("Religion wants the mother to pass the day at home in order that she may fulfill her high and holy mission toward her husband and her children"), and a family-sustaining wage.[12] In the encyclical *Quanta cura* (1864), Pope Pius IX first cited the vital place of the family in a valid worldly order, a theme reinforced by new emphasis in lay devotion to the Virgin and the Holy Family.[13]

These currents converged in Pope Leo XIII's 1893 encyclical *Rerum novarum,* or *The Condition of Labor.* Leo warned about the dangers of state displacement of the family. Children, he said, were "a kind of extension of the father's person", and the

---

[11] See John D. Callahan, *The Catholic Attitude toward a Familial Minimum Wage* (Washington, DC: Catholic University of America, 1936), 13–24; and James Healy, S.J., *The Just Wage, 1750–1890: A Study of Moralists from Saint Alphonsus to Leo XIII* (The Hague: Martinus Nijhoff, 1966), 172, 187, 298, 350–52, 461–62.

[12] From John A. Ryan and Joseph Husslein, *The Church and Labor* (New York: Macmillan, 1920), 4, 10–19, 44–49.

[13] See Colleen McDannell, *The Christian Home in Victorian America, 1840–1900* (Bloomington: Indiana University Press, 1986), 13–16.

family as an institution had existence and rights prior to those of the state. It was "a great and pernicious error", he added, for government to intervene into the privacy of homes. Accordingly, Leo emphasized the moral obligation of employers to pay a wage rooted in natural justice, an obligation "greater and more ancient than the free consent of contracting parties, namely that the wage shall not be less than enough to support a worker who is thrifty and upright". He did not, at this time, directly affirm the family wage ideal. But his indirect references (e.g., "If a worker receives a wage sufficiently large to enable him to provide comfortably for himself, his wife, and his children, he will, if prudent, gladly strive to practice thrift") strongly suggested the familial nature of the desired wage.[14]

The secular labor union movement also embraced the family wage as the measure of justice, to be secured through organization. In the United States, the National Trades Union condemned maternal and child labor in 1836, arguing that under such conditions "the parent, the husband, or the brother is deprived of a sufficient subsistence to support himself and family, when without the auxiliary aid of the female, by his own labor alone he might have supported himself and family in decency and kept his wife or relative at home." The labor publication *Ten Hour Advocate* editorialized in 1846 that "we hope the day is not distant when the husband will be able to provide for his wife and family, without sending the former to ensure the drudgery of a cotton mill." Speaking in 1898 for the American Federation of Labor, Samuel Gompers claimed for workers "a living wage — which when expended in an economic manner shall be sufficient to maintain an average-sized family in a manner consistent with whatever the contemporary local civilization recognizes as indispensable to physical and mental health". The *Shoe Workers' Journal* defined the just wage as "everything necessary to the life of a normal man . . . the

---

[14] Pope Leo XIII, *Rerum Novarum: Encyclical Letter on the Condition of Labor* (Washington, DC: National Catholic Welfare Conference, 1942), 10–11, 23–28.

right to marriage, the right to have chidren, and to educate them".[15]

Labor contract demands were increasingly calculated on this family basis, linked to the steady elimination of the employment of married women and children. The United Mine Workers made its case before the U.S. Bituminous Coal Commission in 1919 on the "family of five" standard. Miners advanced the same claim in 1920 arbitration proceedings for the anthracite coal industry. In 1926, the Baltimore and Ohio Railroad reached agreement with its unions specifying that no married women whose husbands had jobs would be employed by the company. The Union Pacific Railroad, under union pressures, also dismissed most married female employees, replacing them with men.

Some unorthodox American corporate leaders imbibed the voluntary family wage spirit. For example, in a stunning 1914 action, Henry Ford announced that he was immediately doubling the minimum rate paid most autoworkers to $5.00 for eight hours of work.

Significantly, only employees in specific household forms would qualify for this wage: "All married men living with and taking good care of their families"; single men age 23 and over with "proven thrifty habits"; and men under age 23 and women "who are the sole support of some next-of-kin as blood relative". Complementing this approach, the company refused to hire married women with employable husbands. Ford retained a phalanx of "social investigators" to visit workers' homes and ensure compliance.

In justifying his wage program, Ford emphasized that "[i]t would be bad morals to go back to the old market rate of paying." The wage should be seen as carrying all of the worker's obligations outside the shop. If only the individual was concerned, the calculation of needs would be simple: "But he is

[15] Quotations from James Boyle, *The Minimum Wage and Syndicalism* (Cincinnati: Stewart and Kidd, 1913), 73; and Martha May, "The Historical Problem of the Family Wage: The Ford Motor Company and the Five Dollar Day", *Feminist Studies* 8 (Summer 1978): 401–2.

not just an individual. . . . He is a householder. He is perhaps a father with children who must be reared to usefulness on what he is able to earn." The work of mothers must also be recognized, Ford said: "The man does the work in the shop, but his wife does the work in the home. The shop must pay them both." The alternative, he concluded, was "the hideous prospect of little children and their mothers being forced out to work". [16]

The voluntary effort to construct a family wage took a different shape in France and offered useful lessons. Child allowances had a long history there, particularly in military and civil service pay schedules. After 1900, though, an alternate approach emerged. Under Roman Catholic tutelage, study circles including French business leaders generated new interest in private family allowance programs. In 1916, the large Joya Engineering Works at Grenoble—through the decision of its manager, M. Romanet—introduced a family allowance scheme for its workers in which an extra sum determined according to his number of dependent children was added to the man's base salary. With the additional stimuli of war and inflation, the concept spread swiftly. In 1918, most railway workers and miners came under allowance programs, and other industries followed. To counter the possibility that some employers would avoid paying extra wages by refusing to hire men with children, family advocates created an ingenious private system of "district equalization funds". Instead of paying allowances directly to employees, employers now made a regular contribution, set by the total number of workers in the firm, to a regional fund, which then distributed the allowances. By the mid-1920s, these funds also offered private family services such as midwives, visiting nurses, vacation centers, birth and breastfeeding bonuses, layettes, medical centers, and milk for children. [17]

[16] Henry Ford in collaboration with Samuel Crawther, *My Life and Work* (Garden City, NY: Doubleday, 1922), 116, 123; and May, "Historical Problem of the Family Wage", 409–14.

[17] See Robert Talmy, *Histoire du mouvement familial en France, 1896–1939* (n.p.: Union Nationale de Caisses d'allocations Familiales, 1962).

3. *Building a State-Coerced Family Wage*

Despite these attempts at voluntary action, the dominant tendency was toward the use of government to limit market forces in order to construct a family wage economy.

The earliest systematic effort having this goal was in Australia, where a campaign against "sweating", or piecework in the home, served as midwife to the modern minimum wage movement. Under mounting public pressure generated by reports of "scandalous exploitation" of women and children, the parliament of the state of Victoria approved the "Factories and Shops Act of 1896". This statute created elective boards in six industries with the power to set minimum wage rates. The concept spread quickly to other industries and states and had the idea of a "living family wage" at its core. Distinctive features of the Australian system were its "discrediting of the principle of equal pay for equal work" in the name of social justice and the goal of social order. As Commonwealth Justice Henry Bournes Higgins put the issue: "One cannot conceive of industrial peace unless the employee has secured to him wages sufficient for the essentials of human existence."

In his 1907 "Harvester Judgment", which governed Australian wage boards until 1934, Higgins chose a family "of approximately five" and a daily male wage of seven shillings as the wage "necessary to allow the average man to live his life according to Australian standards". This measure of the normal Australian life specifically included marriage and children. Concerning women, Higgins said that they "are not usually legally responsible for maintenance of a family", and so should be paid only at an individual level. Over time, the wage courts generally settled on a female wage that was 54 percent of that paid men. Commentators saw "no precise reason" for this figure, because no systematic study of the issue had ever been conducted. Higgins did recognize the potential market problem of driving men out of work through the lower wage paid women. He resolved it by falling back on a gender-based division of labor: "Where a certain kind of work was recognized as men's work, then women who were employed to do that work should be paid the same wages as the men"; in "women's trades", meanwhile, the lower, nonfamily rate would prevail.

This attempt to circumvent market forces through state control of wages and job categories was generally popular. Indeed, by 1922, Higgins could boast that "[t]he system is now . . . universally accepted as just and proper." Yet his confidence papered over a host of problems. To begin with, micromanagement of household budgets remained a standing temptation, with union petitions and court decisions laying out precise Australian family budgets covering everything from "union fees and one newspaper" to "tobacco and drink". Second, the assumption of a normal family of five proved inefficient and delivered a gross overpayment to labor. Under the system, childless men made out quite well, whereas families with five or more children fell far short of a true "living wage". On the basis of 1 million adult male laborers in early-twentieth-century Australia, 3 million children were sustained by the basic minimum wage. In truth, the nation had only 900,000 children, which forced industry to support 2.1 million hypothetical dependents. Third, the "single" standard for women proved overly simplistic, with some estimates suggesting that 20 percent of female laborers had children dependent on them for their primary support.

In addition, market forces could not be wholly contained within gender-segregated job categories, and significant distortions emerged. While the central goals of the scheme were to reduce the labor of children and married women, the results often ran contrary. One study of the clothing and furniture trades in Victoria, for example, found that the minimum rates had two immediate results: a great increase in juvenile and women employees and growing complaints over the scarcity of really competent adult laborers. In the clothing industry, men enjoying the higher rate were driven from the field. Although the researcher suggested that "this is hardly a cause for complaint as the trade is legitimately a woman's trade", he did worry over the manufacturing business lost to other sites "through the inability to execute orders owing to lack of skilled [female] labor". In the boot trade, too, highly paid men found themselves displaced by women. Indeed, the number of women and children employed in 1911 was an astonishing four times greater than in 1896.[18]

Such flawed results did little to discourage other English-speaking nations from turning to the familial minimum wage as an instrument of social justice. In Great Britain, the Fabian socialist Sidney Webb praised the Australian defense of the family economy. He contrasted the need to provide for "competent male adult workers at a full Standard Rate" with the "persistent desire" of employers to use "boy labor, girl labor, married women's labor, the labor of old men, of the feeble-minded, [and] of the decrepit and brokendown invalids". He considered work in the latter categories to be "parasitic" on the community, since these persons could draw on the support of others: "The employer of adult women . . . pays them a wage insufficient to keep them in full efficiency, irrespective of what they receive from their parents, husbands, or lovers." Webb thought it necessary to set different minimum wages for men and women, in order to defend the community against the economic parasitism of "the marginal woman". Under the force of such arguments, Britain's Trade Boards Act of 1903 set up,

[18] This discussion of the Australian minimum wage is derived from Henry Bournes Higgins, *A New Province for Law and Order* (London and Sydney: Constable & Co., 1922), 95–97; E. M. Burns, *Wages and the State: A Comparative Study of the Problems of State Wage Regulation* (London: P. S. King & Son, 1926); Mary T. Rankin, *Arbitration and Conciliation in Australia* (London: Allen & Unwin, 1916), 101–5; Paul Stanley Collier, *Minimum Wage Legislation in Australia* (Albany, NY: J. B. Lyon, 1915), 1906–10, 2088–91; Orwell de R. Foenander, *Towards Industrial Peace in Australia* (Melbourne: Melbourne University Press, 1937), 69–74, 85–86; and George Anderson, *Fixation of Wages in Australia* (Melbourne: Macmillan, 1929), 188–207.

in selected industries, Australian-styled wage boards with the power to establish familial minimum wages.[19]

In the United States, the minimum wage movement took new moral life through publication in 1906 of Father John Ryan's *A Living Wage.* Although rooted in the wage and justice concepts found in *Rerum novarum,* Ryan's work also exhibited new respect for secular socialist theory (his introduction gives "especial acknowledgment" to the British socialists Sidney and Beatrice Webb and John A. Hobson) and waning concern about the danger posed by the state to family autonomy.

Ryan stressed the need to "moralize" the wage contract. He criticized America's "cult of individual freedom" and rejected, as a pipe dream, a regime of natural liberty that would maintain at all times the greatest possible amount of happiness. Instead, Ryan declared that "the laborer has a right to a family Living Wage because this is the only way in which he can exercise his right to the means of maintaining a family, and he has a right to these means because they are an essential condition of normal life." This right, he continued, was a right in the full Catholic understanding of that phrase. Nature and reason, he argued, had decreed that the family should be supported by its head. Even unmarried males should receive a familial wage as a right, so as to make a necessary provision for subsequent marriage. At the same time, the welfare of society rendered it "imperative that the wife and mother should not engage in any labor except that of the household". Ryan concluded that these moral obligations were so pressing that "the State has both the right and the duty to compel all employers to pay a Living Wage."[20]

[19] See Sidney Webb, *The Economic Theory of a Legal Minimum Wage* (New York: National Consumer's League, 1913), 14–21; John A. Ryan, S.T.D., *A Living Wage: Its Ethical and Economic Aspects* (New York: Macmillan, 1910), 4–37, 110–37, 301.

[20] John A. Ryan, *Distributive Justice: The Right and Wrong of Our Present Distribution of Wealth* (New York: Macmillan, 1916), 374–76.

Ryan helped kindle a new Catholic activism in favor of so-cial intervention by the state. In subsequent works such as *Distributive Justice* (1916) and *Social Reconstruction* (1920), Ryan made more explicit the role of government in bending market forces to shore up the faltering natural economy of the traditional family. Within this context, he repeatedly emphasized that "the support of the family falls properly upon the husband and father, not upon the wife and mother"; that "marriage is essential to normal life for the great majority of men", and that women had moral claim only to a wage sufficient to maintain one person.[21]

Pope Pius XI's 1931 encyclical *Quadragesimo anno* showed a similar shift in emphasis. Explicitly demanding a family wage for every adult male worker, the encyclical avoided many of Leo XIII's cautions about the ambitions of the state and called instead for governmental reforms to guarantee just such a wage.[22] Other commentators from the period emphasized the sweeping nature of these demands. As one Jesuit writer put it:

> [I]t will be absolutely necessary to see to it that female labor is kept from the labor market, something that will have to be attained by prudent and clear-sighted measures. Everyone knows that this cannot be accomplished by decree but requires a far-reaching reconstruction of the entire economic system. . . . This economic change must, therefore, be demanded with all moral arguments. Social justice puts force behind these moral arguments.[23]

Properly secularized, these were the same justifications that underlay the progressive reform campaign to restrict the labor of women and children. Articulate voices, such as those of John

---

[21] Ibid., and John A. Ryan, *Social Reconstruction* (New York: Macmillan, 1920), 74–75.

[22] Pope Pius XI, *Quadragesimo Anno,* in *Two Basic Social Encyclicals* (Washington, DC: Catholic University of America Press, 1943), 133–35.

[23] Oswald von Nell-Brenning, S.J., *Reorganization of Social Economy: The Social Encyclical Developed and Explained* (New York: Bruce, 1939), 176–77.

Spargo and Annie Daniel, blasted an economic system that employed over one million married women, "87 percent" of whom worked solely for "reason of poverty arising from low wages, frequent unemployment, or sickness of their husbands". They said that working mothers were responsible for "numerous evils", including the malnourishment of children, infant mortality, and crime. In his progressive phase, Theodore Roosevelt declared that "no nation can exist at all unless the average woman is a homekeeper, the good wife, and unless she is the mother of a sufficient number of healthy children to insure the race going forward and not backward." The progressive poet Edwin Markham described "golden boys and girls" in factories who were "mangled, mind, body, and soul, and aborted into a maturity robbed of power and promise". The American god, Commerce, sat on a pyramid of skulls and had "a measureless Maw that must be continually crammed with the youth and strength and virtue and joy of our children". Working family homes, he said, had become little more than "joyless shanties for bolting down food or snatching a little sleep".[24]

In 1909, bills appeared in several states that would have set a general minimum wage rate, with "substantial agreement" that it be keyed to "a living wage". Yet by 1911, the campaign shifted to a focus exclusively on minimums for women and children. American labor unions, it turned out, opposed legal minimum wages for men, arguing that "[t]hrough organization the wages of men can and will be maintained at a higher minimum than they would be if fixed by legal enactment." At the same time, the unions looked on women workers as a hopeless problem and concluded that legal minimum rates for women and children "would exclude from industry that great body of inexperienced temporary women workers who are partly supported from sources other than their wages, and who, there-

[24] John Spargo, *The Bitter Cry of the Children* (New York: Macmillan, 1906), 34–42, 49; *The Works of Theodore Roosevelt,* vol. 21 (New York: Scribner's, 1925), 145; and Edwin Markham, *Children in Bondage* (New York: Hearst's International Library, 1914), 15, 37–39, 58–59, 67–71.

fore, demoralize the entire wage system". In addition, there was general agreement among legal scholars that universal minimum wage legislation would violate constitutional "due process" guarantees. Since women must bear the children for their generation, though, the scholars also concurred that they could be legitimately protected in labor matters through the police powers of the state.[25]

With the Australian example plainly in view, in 1912 the Massachusetts legislature enacted the first minimum wage statute. It established a commission and subordinate wage boards to set minimum rates for minors and adult women. Over the next few years, another ten states with progressive majorities — including Wisconsin, California, Minnesota, and Oregon — enacted similar laws. All were predicated on the belief that the female minimum wage should be calculated on an "individual" rather than a family basis. The broader goal was defense of the family. As the prize-winning essay in a National Industrial Conference competition put it, minimum wage legislation

> can only be justified by the social necessity of protecting the family. The woman is the mother and trainer of children. She is the ridge pole of the family structure. . . . The male has been the head of the family and principal breadwinner since the dawn of civilization. . . . Women and children of the families of able-bodied male workers have no legitimate place in industry.[26]

Even the rhetoric of rights came to be officially employed. Echoing Father Ryan, the National War Labor Board, in setting out principles to settle industrial disputes during World War I, stated: "The right of all workers . . . to a living wage

[25] "Position of the American Federation of Labor on the Legal Minimum Wage", Appendix III in Irene Osgood Andrews, *Minimum Wage Legislation* (Albany, NY: J. B. Lyon, 1914), 82–83; and Harleigh Hartman, *Should the State Interfere in the Determination of Wage Rates?* (New York: National Industrial Conference Board, 1920), 65.

[26] Hartman, *Should the State Interfere?* 78.

is hereby declared. . . . [M]inimum rates of pay shall be established which will insure the subsistence of the worker and his family in health and reasonable comfort."[27]

Opposing this push for minimum rates was a coalition of business leaders and feminists. Since 1904, the National Association of Manufacturers (NAM) had defended, as among its goals, both individualism and equal rights: "The social and material welfare of all classes of people is dependent upon the full exercise of individual freedom consistent with the equal rights of all." The organization emphasized that "no limitation should be placed upon the opportunities of any person to learn any trade to which he or she may be adapted."[28] For their own reasons, feminist members of the National Woman's Party also supported equal work and pay for women outside the home and a laissez faire approach to labor legislation. There were even rumors circulating among progressive and union circles that NAM funded the National Woman's Party.[29] Whatever the relationship, the two organizations jointly cheered the U.S. Supreme Court's 1923 decision in *Adkins* v. *Children's Hospital* that struck down state minimum wage statutes as a violation of the due process clause of the Fifth Amendment. Tipping the hat to the advocates of a free labor market, the court found such laws to be no more than price-fixing schemes. For the feminists, the court found that the differences between men and women "have now come almost, if not quite, to the vanishing

[27] Quoted in Felix Frankfurter, *District of Columbia Minimum Wage Cases: Brief for Appeals* (New York: Charles Young, n.d. [1921?]), 134–35.

[28] From John Nellis Stalker, Jr., "The Americanism of the National Association of Manufacturers", master's thesis (Madison: University of Wisconsin, 1947), 118; and Albion Guilforn Taylor, "Labor Policies of the National Association of Manufacturers", *University of Illinois Studies in the Social Sciences* 15 (March 1928): 38.

[29] Noted in Lillian Holmen Mohr, *Frances Perkins* (n.p.: North River Press, 1979), 192; and Mary Anderson and Mary N. Winslow, *Women at Work: The Autobiography of Mary Anderson* (Minneapolis: University of Minnesota Press, 1951), 171.

point" and could no longer justify state regulation of wages based on gender.[30]

The reformers' push for a family wage in the United States gained new momentum during the New Deal. Central figures in this campaign were so-called social feminists such as Secretary of Labor Frances Perkins, Women's Bureau Chief Mary Anderson, and Mary Dewson of the Democratic National Committee. As bitter opponents of both the business associations and the National Woman's Party, these New Dealers saw the achievement of a family wage as the solution to many social problems. They believed that although working mothers should be treated as equals to men in the workplace, maternal labor was clearly an undesirable social goal. Moreover, with legal scholar Barbara Armstrong, they agreed that "[t]here can be no dispute that it is today assumed that a male worker's wage should be a family wage rather than an individual wage."[31] As Mary Anderson summed it up: "I think the whole thing could be taken care of if the provider for the family got sufficient wages. Then married women would not be obliged to go to work to supplement an inadequate income for their families."[32]

Indeed, there were aspects of the New Deal that could be fairly seen as a form of coercive traditionalism. Under the National Industrial Recovery Act, for example, wage differentials between men and women were first codified. Bans on home work, moreover, were precisely designed to save mothers and their offspring from exploitation and to restore normal homes — "that is, one with a male breadwinner, a housewife, and children".[33] The Fair Labor Standards Act of 1938 empowered the

[30] *Adkin* v. *Children's Hospital* and *Adkins* v. *Willie A. Lyon's,* 261 U.S. 525, nos. 795, 796 (October term 1922).

[31] Barbara Nachtrieb Armstrong, *Insuring the Essentials — Minimum Wage Plus Social Insurance: A Living Wage Program* (New York: Macmillan, 1932), 146–47.

[32] Anderson and Winslow, *Women at Work,* 156–57.

[33] See Eileen Boris, "Regulating Industrial Homework: The Triumph of 'Sacred Motherhood'", *Journal of American History* 71 (March 1985): 749.

federal government to eliminate child labor and to set minimum wages for large categories of workers. There was no gender distinction built into the law, but the implicit goal was to fix a minimum rate that would allow the laborer to sustain a family on one income. Moreover the Social Security system—particularly through the amendments of 1939—was constructed to undergird a family wage economy: child allowances (ADC) for widowed and abandoned mothers and spouse and survivor benefits for the homemaker.

Other actions taken to counter the economic emergency of the 1930s strengthened the family wage system. The strained job situation reinforced the assumptions that men supported families and that women either supported only themselves or supplemented husbands' pay. In 1931, the American Federation of Labor (AFL) adopted a nine-point program to counter unemployment, bemoaning the "unfortunate trend of family life" and urging "preference of employment to those upon whom family or dependency rests". The same year, the president of the Carnegie Institute of Technology argued that working women had "crowded" men out of their "birthright", and proposed that 75 percent of available jobs be reserved for men. Section 213 of the 1932 Federal Economy Act mandated that one spouse quit if both husband and wife were in federal government employ; over 75 percent of those who did so were women.[34]

More direct restrictions on women's labor blossomed among the states. Governors in Alabama, Idaho, Indiana, Pennsylvania, and Rhode Island issued orders restricting the employment of married women. A 1930–31 survey by the National Education Association found that 77 percent of the nation's school districts contacted refused to hire married women as teachers and that 63 percent fired women on their marriage. In Akron,

---

[34] Examples are from Philip S. Foner, *Women and the American Labor Movement: From World War I to the Present* (New York: Free Press, 1980), 257.

Ohio, rubber producers and department store owners complied with a city council request to dismiss female workers with employed husbands and replace them with unemployed men. Nationwide, 43 percent of public utilities reported curbs on the hiring of married women. Popular attitudes stood behind these actions. A Gallup Poll in 1936 found that a hefty 82 percent of all Americans believed that a woman should not work if her husband was employed. [35]

State legislation restricting the type of work that women could do, or the hours they could work, also reached a culmination in this period. Legislators continued to act on the assumption that all women were actual or potential mothers, which transformed their health into a public concern. By 1941, forty-six states banned night work by women in various fields; forty-four had special laws governing the number of hours they could work; and twenty-five mandated special meal and rest periods. [36]

In Europe, by way of comparison, voluntary family allowance programs also succumbed at this time to the temptations of government control. The early 1930s witnessed the transfer of the private French allowance funds to the national government, which was part of a political compromise between the religious movements originally behind the campaign and the socialist–dominated trade unions. The same development occurred in Belgium. Meanwhile, direct state provision of family benefits and child allowances spread throughout the continent, from fascist Italy to social democratic Sweden. In the latter country, though, the socialist intellectuals Alva and Gunnar Myrdal raised a new theme. They argued that the tension between family life and industrial society, between home and work — seen most urgently in rapidly falling birthrates — might be resolved only through the full socialization of childrearing costs. The family wage concept, they said, was no longer rele-

[35] Ibid., 258.
[36] Ibid., 353.

vant. It should be supplanted by a new system in which both men and women were fully and equally part of the paid labor force and in which the state took moral, financial, and even direct responsibility for the care of children.[37]

By 1940, though, these were minority voices on the Western stage. The family wage ideal had triumphed in the United States, large sections of Europe, and the British Commonwealth. Most progressives, social democrats, and reform liberals agreed on the justice of paying an adult man a wage sufficient to support his wife and children and of keeping married women at home. The wage market must be regulated, they assumed, to defend family integrity. Although scattered examples of voluntary efforts to construct a family wage remained, varied use of the state to secure family justice was the dominant theme.

Yet over the next forty years, these systems of reconciling family life to the market unraveled, and the "social factor" in setting wage rates disappeared. The process can be traced most easily in the United States, where it occurred in two phases. The first, from 1942 to 1963, witnessed the dismantling of a direct wage advantage for men. The second and more important phase, from 1964 to the late 1980s, focused on eliminating occupational segregation in America, which had guided individuals into "men's" and "women's" jobs.

World War II, like all modern wars, occasioned social revolution on many fronts, including family and gender relations. Social engineers, emboldened by their experiences during the New Deal, tackled the potential shortage of defense plant workers through a rapid elimination of hiring and pay preferences for men, the most visible manifestations of the family wage. Federal officials took the first steps in February 1942, when the National War Production Board proclaimed the "immediate extension of defense training to women on a basis of equality with the training of men". At the same time, the Joint Planning

---

[37] Alva Myrdal and Gunnar Myrdal, *Kris I Befolkningsfrågan* (Stockholm: Bonniers, 1934).

Board opened up "Lanham Act" day-care centers to the children of working mothers. Proponents of the family wage ideal, such as Labor Secretary Frances Perkins, raised a brief defense of the existing order. As she wrote in June 1942, to Katherine Lenroot of the Children's Bureau: "What are you doing to prevent the spread of the day nursery system, which I regard as the most unfortunate reaction to the hysterical propaganda about recruiting women workers?" Yet this approach was quickly routed. In November 1942, the National War Labor Board (NWLB) issued General Order Number 16, the death knell of the intentional family wage. It encouraged employers to increase wages for women being paid less than men "for comparable quality and quantity of work on the same or similar operations". By January 1944, over two thousand employers reported making such adjustments, reflecting both the extent of purposeful discrimination before Pearl Harbor and the revolutionary consequence of the war.[38]

Another change stimulated in wartime through government pressure was scientific job evaluation. In 1923, passage of the Classification Act introduced a pay structure to the federal Civil Service, where salary was fixed through a systematic analysis of duties and responsibilities that disregarded the gender of the employee. For the next two decades, though, the overwhelming majority of private businesses continued to set wage rates through some combination of market forces, collective bargaining agreements, and cultural assumptions about the relative family obligations of men and women.

With the war emergency again as the justification, the NWLB encouraged scientific job evaluation in all defense plants. A November 1945 NWLB ruling, for example, gave approval to "the principle of a single evaluation line for all jobs in a plant regardless of whether the jobs are performed by men or women".

[38] See Walter Fogel, *The Equal Pay Act: Implications for Comparable Worth* (New York: Praeger, 1984), 8, 14, 20; and Foner, *Women and the American Labor Movement*, 348–54.

The consequences of this federal pressure were striking. A survey by the National Industrial Conference Board found that whereas only 13 percent of firms had used this technique in 1939, a hefty 57 percent did so by 1947.[39]

American labor unions also entered a time of confused, war-induced retreat from the family wage ideal. As a joint United Auto Workers (UAW)–Congress on Industrial Organization (CIO) convention resolution in 1944 put it: "The war has been instrumental in bringing forward women as never before in all phases of our national life." While the American Federation of Labor (AFL) dragged its feet on issues of equal pay for equal work, child care, and maternity leave, the UAW and CIO quickly embraced a fairly broad feminist agenda, including pledges to recruit women for positions of union leadership. Once again, federal pressure through the Women's Bureau and the National War Labor Board proved instrumental in effecting this transformation.[40]

After the war and through the early 1960s, labor union pronouncements exhibited a kind of schizophrenia about women's labor and some lingering respect for the family wage regime. At their 1946 joint convention, the CIO-UAW attacked management's desire to recruit female employees, blasting the tendency "to use women workers to lower wages of all workers, to weaken the Union seniority system, and generally to destroy labor Unions". Yet in 1949, and again in 1953, management was blamed for the very opposite tendency—a refusal to recruit women "by spreading propaganda against women working".

[39] J. E. Buckley, "Equal Pay in America", in *Equal Pay for Women: Progress and Problems in Seven Countries,* ed. Barrie O. Pettman (Bradford, England: MCB Books, 1975), 42; Fogel, *Equal Pay Act,* 15; Foner, *Women and the American Labor Movement,* 356.

[40] "UAW-CIO Convention, 1944, Resolutions No. 8 and No. 9", in UAW Women's Department, *UAW Policy Established by Convention Resolutions Relative to Women Workers' Rights* (1969?), 23–24; Foner, *Women and the American Labor Movement,* 374–76.

Similar internal union disputes surrounded the questions of an Equal Pay Law, protective legislation, and the Equal Rights Amendment. The AFL consistently opposed a federal law guaranteeing equal pay for equal work, first proposed in 1945, whereas the CIO and the UAW endorsed it. Only when the organizations merged in 1957 did the latter position win out. However, the proposed Equal Rights Amendment, with its feminist-capitalist pedigree dating from the 1920s, drew regular scorn from most union leadership through the mid-1960s. As a 1959 UAW resolution explained: "We continue to oppose and expose the so-called, but mis-named, Equal Rights Amendment, whose title is about as meaningful as the one that is bestowed on right-to-work bills."

Beneath the surface of this general confusion was evidence of continuing rank-and-file opposition to women workers. In 1946, for example, the UAW blasted the tendency of its own locals to retain clauses in their charters "which openly discriminate against women in the Union". Other documents and resolutions stressed the need to "educate" union members about the "emerging" roles of women. [41]

By the late 1940s, direct pay discrimination in favor of men within individual firms — the core conception behind an open family wage system — had become relatively rare, a social casualty of World War II. As an analysis by labor economist Victor Fuchs showed, there was no evidence by 1959/60 "that employer discrimination is a major direct influence upon male-female differentials in average hourly earnings". Nonetheless, the push for a Federal Equal Pay Act took on growing symbolic importance. First introduced in Congress in 1945, the measure won endorsement from President Dwight Eisenhower in his 1956 State of the Union Address. As noted above, opposition by the AFL ended in 1957. One of John Kennedy's

[41] *UAW Policy Established by Convention Resolutions,* 13–15, 18, 21–24; James J. Kenneally, *Women and American Trade Unions* (St. Albans, VT: Eden Press Women's Publications, 1978), 178–86.

first acts, on assuming the presidency in 1961, was to create a President's Commission on the Status of Women, which heartily endorsed the proposed Equal Pay Act. During hearings held in 1962, little evidence could be produced showing direct wage discrimination against women within individual firms. The apparent fact that the measure would have little effect was probably the key to its passage in 1963.

Despite these developments, the celebrated "wage gap" between men and women actually grew between 1939 and 1960. In the former year, median female earnings were 59.29 percent of male's; by 1966, the figure had fallen to 53.66 percent (curiously close to the 54 percent established by Australian wage courts fifty years earlier). This occurred even though the proportion of females with earned incomes climbed from 39.2 percent in 1947 to 61 percent in 1966. [42] Although direct wage discrimination in favor of men had virtually vanished, another factor had more than compensated for that change and had effectively restored — even strengthened — the informal family wage system. This factor was job segregation: the cultural recognition of "male" and "female" jobs.

A detailed analysis of gender differentiation in employment in this period by economist Vernon Clover appeared in 1970 and helps explain the peculiar dynamics. Part of the explanation lay in the declining proportion of women working "full time" relative to "part time". In 1950, 64.4 percent of employed women worked an average of 35 or more hours a week; by 1965, only 58.9 percent. More significant, though, was the crowding of women into employment categories that were over 90 percent female: file clerks, key punch operators, secretaries, stenographers, typists, and so on. Meanwhile, women actually lost ground in "men's" job categories (defined as an occupational group more than 95 percent male): auditors, at-

[42] Peter J. Sloane, *Women and Low Pay* (London: Macmillan, 1980), 238; Victor R. Fuchs, "Differences in Hourly Earnings between Men and Women", *Monthly Labor Review* 94 (May 1971): 14; Kenneally, *Women and American Trade Unions,* 178–89; and Buckley, "Equal Pay in America", 44.

torneys, chemists, engineers, and draftsmen. In 1947, for example, 7.2 percent of employed married women were managers and proprietors; by 1966, only 4.8 percent. Similarly, whereas 25.6 percent of all employed married women were factory workers in 1947, only 17.2 percent were in 1966. By way of contrast, the growth sectors for women's employment were in office and "service" work. In 1947, 21.2 percent of employed married women were clerical workers; by 1966, 31.4 percent. "Service" sector employment accounted for 11.2 percent of married women workers in 1947, rising to 15.5 percent in 1966. Not coincidentally, it seems, clerical workers enjoyed the smallest increase in average salary during the 1960s (of thirteen occupational groups surveyed), whereas chemists and chief accountants recorded the highest. As Clover concludes: "The traditional social taboos against females in certain kinds of occupations and levels of responsibility are evidently stronger than is commonly realized."[43] Indeed, the passing of overt wage discrimination in favor of men seems to have been fully compensated for by a more subtle cultural distortion of the labor market.

Of course, these "taboos" , or normative social mores, surfaced in other ways as well. For example, Ferdinand Lundberg's and Marynia Farnham's 1947 bestseller, *Modern Women: The Lost Sex,* blasted feminist pretensions to male roles: "A female who attempts to achieve masculinity is psychically ill in the same way as a male who attempts to achieve femininity." Alice K. Leopold, Eisenhower's director of the Women's Bureau, publicly urged working women to go home. "After all," she stated at a news conference, "the most important function of a woman is to run a home, be a mother, and contribute to the life of her family and community." In 1956, *Life* magazine published a special issue on "The American Woman". Featured was an essay

[43] Vernon T. Clover, *Changes in Differences in Earnings and Occupational Status of Men and Women, 1947–1967* (Lubbock: Department of Economics, College of Business Administration, Texas Tech University, 1970), 4, 17–21, 26–27, 36, 43, 50–51.

by anthropologist Margaret Mead, arguing that the ideal family life in America was one where the wife did not work. The home was still, "as it has been through the ages, women's natural habitat". Another article, by Robert Coughlan, labeled feminism "as quaint as linen dusters and high buttoned shoes", yet an ideology with one fatal historical consequence: "the career women". He also called women home: "If they are feminine women, with truly feminine attitudes, they will . . . accept their wifely functions with good humor and pleasure."[44]

However, these attitudes, and the purposeful distortions of the labor market they maintained, were effectively destroyed by government actions in 1964 and later. The triggering event in this second phase of deconstruction of the family wage was the addition of the word *sex* to Title VII of the Civil Rights Act of 1964. Ironically, this occurred as something of a joke.

The proposed Civil Rights Act had been crafted originally to deal with specific problems facing black Americans, including their ability to vote, to gain equal access to public schools, to utilize public accommodations, and to enjoy equal job opportunities. Title VII, dealing with job issues, would have made it illegal for employers of fifteen or more to discriminate against persons in their hiring, firing, or terms of employment due to race, color, religion, or national origin. Employers could not segregate or classify employees through these categories, nor discriminate in matters of promotions and assignments, wages and benefits, or training and retraining. Similarly, labor unions would be prohibited from basing membership or apprentice programs on such criteria. Title VII also would create the Equal Employment Opportunity Commission (EEOC), with the power to enforce the title's provisions.

On its path to passage, though, a curious development occurred. During debate on the measure in the U.S. House of

---

[44] From Ferdinand Lundberg and Marynia F. Farnham, *Modern Woman: The Lost Sex* (New York: Harper & Brothers, 1947), 92; Leopold quoted in Kennally, *Women and American Trade Unions,* 181; and "The American Woman", *Life,* December 24, 1956, pp. 27, 110, 116.

Representatives, "Dixiecrat" Howard Smith offered an amendment to add the word *sex* to the list of prohibited discriminations found in Title VII. Some believe that his strategy was to load the bill with enough confused and uncertain measures so as to kill it. (Subsequent developments suggest that he may have dimly realized that the surest way to undermine Title VII was to swamp its intended target, black males [about 5 percent of the population], with an equal legal focus on white women [45 percent of the population].) His colleagues greeted the amendment with gales of laughter, yet he assured them that he was "serious about this thing". After faltering debate, the amendment was adopted. Significantly, no hearings were held to gauge the effect of this substantial shift in the measure's purpose and coverage. The amendment survived a conference with the Senate (which also never debated the issue or purpose of putting *sex* in Title VII) and became law. [45]

With this change, the Civil Rights Act of 1964 cut at the heart of job segregation by sex and began the dismantling of America's residual family wage. Title VII eliminated sex as a criterion for entry into any job or firm (with a very few exceptions) and specified that equally productive workers must receive the same wage regardless of their sex. For a few years, the full impact of the measure was unclear. In 1967, though, President Lyndon Johnson began pressing for a more rapid pace of change by issuing Executive Order 11375, which prohibited the federal government and governmental contractors and subcontractors from discriminating in employment on the basis of sex and mandated "affirmative", "result oriented" measures to eliminate job segregation by sex. Between 1968 and 1971, according to one sympathetic commentator, the EEOC "converted Title VII into a magna carta for female workers, grafting to it a set of rules and regulations that certainly could not have passed Congress in 1964, and perhaps not a decade later,

---

[45] See Buckley, "Equal Pay in America", 45–46.

either."[46] Among these actions was an EEOC ruling in August 1969, stating that the provisions of Title VII took precedence over the state laws giving special protections to working women:

> The Commission believes that such State laws and regulations, although originally promulgated for the purpose of protecting females, have ceased to be relevant to our technology or to the expanding role of the female worker in our economy. The Commission has found that such laws and regulations do not take into account the capacities, preferences, and abilities of individual females, and tend to discriminate rather than protect.[47]

Some labor unions began the regular denunciation of both their male members and those labor laws and standards once seen as the embodiment of prolabor goals. The United Auto Workers fell quickly into line with feminist tenets. At its 1966 convention, the UAW instituted programs "to better acquaint our male members with the problems of women workers, the importance of women in the work force, the need for their intensified activity in the community and political life . . . [etc.]". This union's Women's Department praised Johnson's 1967 Executive Order as a sign of the federal government's readiness to proceed "on all fronts to provide the machinery for erasing job discrimination against women". In 1968, the same department played an instrumental role in the founding of the National Organization for Women (NOW), which pledged "to take action to bring women into full partnership in the mainstream of American society now, exercising all the privileges and responsibilities thereof in truly equal partnership with men". The same year, the UAW actually attacked all state laws and regulations granting special protections to working women.

---

[46] Donald Allen Robinson, "Two Movements in Pursuit of Equal Employment Opportunity", *Signs: Journal of Women in Culture and Society* 4, no. 3 (1979): 427.

[47] Quoted in Buckley, "Equal Pay in America", 47.

Calling them "obsolete", the organization condemned "laws which arbitrarily treat women as a separate group with certain stereotyped characteristics, and we oppose particularly the abuse of such laws to the economic detriment of women workers."[48]

The AFL-CIO, however, did raise one last, faltering defense of some aspects of the family wage system. While generally receptive to the protections afforded racial minorities through the Civil Rights Act of 1964, the organization evidenced a continuing reluctance to battle discrimination on the basis of sex. Through 1969, official union periodicals still carried articles that assumed the normal woman's role to be that of a homemaker. AFL-CIO conventions continued to endorse protective legislation for women, and to defend such measures from EEOC scrutiny. Many trade unions found themselves in direct conflict with the EEOC over sexual equality. The Communications Workers of America, for example, battled the government action against American Telephone and Telegraph. The Department of Labor's order that the firm pay $15 million to women and minorities in compensation for "pervasive and systematic discrimination" sparked union complaints that the settlement infringed on collective bargaining rights. A similar struggle ensued after the Civil Rights Commission accused fifteen building trade unions and the Teamsters of pervasive discrimination against women and minorities. Throughout this period, the AFL-CIO also continued to oppose the proposed Equal Rights Amendment. When the measure passed the House of Representatives in 1970, on a 352 to 15 vote, union opposition was instrumental in killing off the measure in the Senate.

Over the next several years, intense feminist pressure focused on the AFL-CIO. In 1972, disgruntled California unionists created Union WAGE (Women's Alliance to Gain Equality),

---

[48] *UAW Policy Established by Convention Resolutions,* 2, 6; and UAW Women's Department, *Report: 1968 Constitutional Convention,* pamphlet (1969?), 1–2, 9.

which labeled unions the "last bastion of male supremacy" and pledged "to raise the consciousness of male unionists". When the ERA came up for another House of Representatives vote in October 1971, an increasing number of independent trade unions had deserted the AFL-CIO position and urged adoption of the measure. Following House approval, the Senate passed the measure in March 1972, on an 84 to 8 vote, after which union opposition to the march of sexual equality collapsed. Delegates to the AFL-CIO's 1973 convention voted to support the ERA as "a symbol of commitment to equal opportunity for women and equal status for women". By 1975, the feminist triumph within the unions was virtually complete, with the AFL-CIO pledging to support the ERA, to battle against all forms of sexual discrimination at the bargaining table, to support child-care legislation and maternity leave protection, to open all apprenticeship programs to women, and to strengthen the union's own Civil Rights Department. The century-old effort by American working men to create and defend a family wage structure had come to an end.[49]

The practical effects of this second phase of deconstruction of the family wage can be documented. A careful analysis in 1978 by economist Andrea Beller found that EEOC investigations and settlements under Title VII of the Civil Rights Act of 1964 had a decided and measurable effect. Between 1967 and 1974, she reported, these enforcement measures directly narrowed the male-female earnings differential by 14 percent in the private sector, by 2 percent in the governmental sector, and by 7 percent in the economy as a whole.[50] More recent work has documented the stagnation or decline in the real wages earned by men, ages 19 through 34, since 1970, in con-

[49] See Kenneally, *Women and American Trade Unions,* 191–99.

[50] Andrea Beller, "Title VII and the Male/Female Earnings Gap: An Economic Analysis", reprint 297 (Madison: Institute for Research on Poverty Research Series, University of Wisconsin, 1979). Originally appeared in *Harvard Women's Law Journal* 1 (1978): 157–73.

trast to a real increase in the wages earned by women in the same age category. [51]

Another way to assess the retreat of the family wage ideal through the American economy as a whole is to look at the income of married-couple households and calculate the income ratio of those with wives in the labor force to those with wives not employed. Such a figure takes neatly into account a whole range of factors: the relative equality of pay and career commitments by men and women, the influence of seniority, the relative usage of part-time work, the pressures of child care, and so on. In a pure "family wage" economy, such a ratio would tend toward 1.00, as law and custom reinforced a higher wage for the male breadwinner. In an economy resting on pure gender equality, such a ratio would tend toward 2.00, as the husband and wife approached complete economic equality in all aspects of their lives and where a one-income couple would be disadvantaged accordingly. The trend in the United States between 1970 and 1988 is summarized in Table 1.

Table 1. Median Monetary Income of Married-Couple Families (in current dollars)

	1970	1975	1980	1985	1987	1988
A. Wife in paid labor force	12,276	17,237	26,879	36,431	40,422	42,709
B. Wife not in paid labor force	9,304	12,752	18,972	24,556	26,652	27,220
Ratio of A/B	1.32	1.35	1.42	1.48	1.52	1.57

Source: Data from *Statistical Abstract of the United States,* 1989, table 726; 1990, table 729.

[51] See Richard K. Vedder, "Shrinking Paychecks: The New Economics of Family Life", *The Family in America* 3 (Jan. 1989): 2–4; and Frank Levy, "We're Running Out of Tricks to Keep Our Prosperity High", *Washington Post,* Dec. 14, 1986, pp. H1, H4.

These figures reflect a dramatic shift, slowly building in the 1970s (an average annual increase in the ratio of 0.010), accelerating in the 1980–85 period (an average annual increase in the ratio of 0.012), and surging after 1985 (an average annual increase in the ratio of 0.030).

It seems safe to conclude that the last remnants of a system designed to protect both the incomes of male breadwinners and the maternal role of women are now disintegrating. The most curious aspect is how little notice and public comment this revolutionary change in family economics has occasioned. From the inclusion of the word *sex* in Title VII of the Civil Rights Act of 1964 as an afterthought, through the collapse of historic labor union strategies in the early 1970s, to the accelerated enforcement of gender equalization statutes in the 1980s, Americans have seen the intimate economics of their family living fundamentally reordered, with scant debate and even less awareness of the consequences for themselves, their children, and generations to come.

Three

The Suburban Strategy

An equally ambitious, if differently targeted, strategy for the reconstruction of family life in the industrial age was the turn to the suburbs. Here, advocates believed, families might thrive in an environment that preserved some vestiges of rural living-space — clean air and a small piece of land — within the urban industrial environment. Although the roots of the suburban strategy lay in the Clapham Sect of late eighteenth-century England (see chapter 2), the use of governmental power to encourage American suburbanization did not come until the early 1930s, the opening years of the Great Depression.

The immediate goal of the New Dealers was to salvage the mortgage market and the construction industry. Toward this end, the Home Owners Loan Corporation, set up in 1933, assumed and refinanced approximately one million existing mortgages. More importantly, the National Housing Act of 1934 created the Federal Housing Administration (FHA), which soon "revolutionized" housing finance. Although not fully realized until the late 1940s, FHA innovations included development of the long-term amortized mortgage featuring a low down payment (prior to 1933, it was rare for a mortgage to cover more than 50 percent of a home's value, or for payments to run more than ten years); the establishment of fairly uniform insurance and property standards for the national housing market; an advance financial and insurance commitment to large-scale developers, which made mass production possible; and technical and land-planning standards that "contributed greatly to more sophisticated builder and tract housing work".[1] Other measures from the period designed to help create an expanding

---

[1] James B. Mason, *History of Housing in the U.S., 1930–1980* (Houston, TX: Gulf, 1982), 13.

mortgage market included creation of the Federal Home Loan Bank in 1932–33 and the chartering of the Federal National Mortgage Association ("Fannie Mae") in 1938.

The reshaping of the federal income tax in this era created indirect subsidies of equal, if not greater, significance. One key decision by Congress was to give preferred treatment to the "imputed rent" of an owner-occupied home. If homeowners had been taxed like other investors, they would have had to count as income the rent they could have obtained on their house, less appropriate deductions for interest, maintenance, and so on. Instead, Congress chose to exclude this imputed income from taxation. At the same time, legislation still allowed taxpayers to take deductions for mortgage interest and state and local property taxes. A further benefit granted was waiver of a capital gains tax on the sale of a house if a new dwelling was purchased within a given period. [2]

Beyond countering the economic emergency of the 1930s, all of these policies enjoyed two justifications. First, policymakers believed that home ownership led to greater citizen responsibility and social stability. Second, and more importantly, they saw housing subsidies as supportive of a unique and desirable family form.

In virtually every discussion of housing policy in the 1933–65 period, the priority of the nuclear family was stressed, an attitude that had deep American roots. At least since the mid-nineteenth century, the detached, rural or suburban, single-family home took a powerful symbolic hold on the American imagination. In the sea of economic uncertainty, the home provided a firm anchor for both adults and children. Popular works such as the Beecher sisters' *The American Woman's Home* (1869) argued for proper home environments that could shape the family's moral character, defend family autonomy, and preserve the basis for a good society. The single-family home

---

[2] See Henry J. Aaron, *Shelter and Subsidies: Who Benefits from Federal Housing Policies?* (Washington, DC: The Brookings Institution, 1972), 53–55.

would be the woman's preserve, while men engaged in the commercial fray. An 1893 painting commissioned by the United States League of Building and Loan Associations, entitled "The American Home, Safeguard of American Liberties", captured this spirit, showing a large family romping before a picturesque three-story home, with a Protestant church, a schoolhouse, and an American flag in the background. Commentators placed great belief in the home as a sturdy bulwark against modern corruptions, giving particular stress to the moral effects of the housing environment. As M. E. W. Sherwood, editor of *Harper's Bazaar,* explained in 1887: "Indiana's divorce laws may be perhaps directly traced to some frightful inharmoniousness in wallpaper. The soothing influence of an Eastlake bookcase on an irritated husband has never been sufficiently calculated."[3]

Influential mid-twentieth-century writers on housing held a similarly strong focus on the family. Glenn Beyer, in *Housing and Society* (1965), stressed that the family "does, after all, constitute the basic unit of residence". Nathan Straus based his 1952 critique of existing housing policy on the family and its needs. Nelson Foote's *Housing Choices and Housing Constraints* (1960) focused on the family as the unit to be housed. Estimates of housing demand, from the 1920s through the mid-1960s, also rested on counts of families, existing or predicted. Housing and family life were, in short, assumed to be two aspects of the same social issue, with the goal being the strengthening of the American home.[4]

[3] See Beecher and Stowe, *The American Woman's Home, or Principles of Domestic Science;* Gwendolyn Wright, *Building the Dream: A Social History of Housing in America* (New York: Pantheon Books, 1981), xv–xvi, 99–109; and M. E. W. Sherwood, "The Mission of Household Art", *Appleton's Journal* 15 (Feb. 5, 1887). Borrowed from Wright.

[4] Glenn H. Beyer, *Housing and Society* (New York: Macmillan, 1965), 44; Nathan Straus, *Two-Thirds of a Nation: A Housing Program* (New York: Knopf, 1952), 4–6; Nelson Foote, *Housing Choices and Housing Constraints* (New York: McGraw-Hill, 1960), 50; and Arnold C. Harberger, *The Demand for Durable Goods* (Chicago: University of Chicago Press, 1960), 90–91.

Declarations of policy intent were equally clear about the place of the family. The key Housing Act of 1949, for instance, stated: "The general welfare and security of the nation and the health and living standards of the people require . . . the realization as soon as feasible of the goal of a decent home and a suitable living environment for every American family." The same theme held as late as 1965, when President Lyndon Johnson declared that "the ultimate goal in our free enterprise system must be a decent home for every American family."

The material triumph of these assumptions also came during the two decades after World War II. As the official "Fannie Mae" history of the period, *The Story of Housing,* explains: "The veterans returned to America after the war with home and family on their minds."[5] The Servicemen's Readjustment Act of 1944 had gone beyond the New Deal programs and had guaranteed home loans for veterans at amounts up to 100 percent of the selling price. Private building had been minimal for over fifteen years, and the average dwelling unit had shrunk in size from 4.8 rooms in the 1920s to 4.26 rooms in the 1940s. As the market responded sluggishly in 1946–47, housing quickly became the central "family issue" facing America. At the 1948 National Conference on Family Life, held in Washington, D.C., the demand for "better housing, more housing, cheaper housing" usurped the whole agenda. President Harry Truman declared to the 900 delegates that "children and dogs are as necessary to the welfare of this country as is Wall Street and the railroads" and urged that pressure be placed on Congress to pass a new housing bill. Conference Chairman Eric Johnston described the lack of decent housing as "one of the great disruptive factors in American family life". The final report explained: "This conference has demonstrated that our homes are decisive influences in family life. No program to strengthen the foundations of

[5] Gertrude Sipperly Fish, ed., *The Story of Housing,* sponsored by the Federal National Mortgage Association (New York: Macmillan, 1979), 472.

family life can overlook the influence of housing, the basic environment of domestic life."[6]

Passage of the controversial Housing Act of 1949 followed, committing the country to providing "a decent home . . . for every American family". The bill authorized $1 billion for slum clearance and a $1.5 billion loan fund to build 810,000 public housing units over six years. Supplemental legislation pumped $1.5 billion into the FHA program and authorized another $1 billion for the Federal National Mortgage Association. This legislation helped stimulate an unprecedented construction boom. In 1949 alone, the industry recorded an unprecedented 1,466,000 housing starts, heavily concentrated in the suburbs. VA and FHA mortgage insurance programs, the "Fannie Mae" history records, "made home ownership available to many families who could never have considered it otherwise. Concentric rings of houses mushroomed up beyond the existing suburbs as suburban sprawl really got rolling." The American middle class now was able "to express its concern for bringing up children in the 'wholesome, clean-air' environment of the suburbs. . . . There was still a symbolism in the single-family-owned suburban home . . . that met the psychological needs of families." Housing officials beamed over "[r]ow after row of almost identical houses, each with a picture window in the living room" to be found on suburban streets, "which were the playgrounds for the numerous small children of the young families which made up the suburban population".[7]

At this level, federal intervention into housing markets seemed a success. Between 1945 and 1960, there was a 90 percent increase in the number of owner-occupied homes. Tax benefits alone, later econometric studies showed, accounted for a substantial share of this increased demand for housing. Put another

---

[6] See "Housing Gets No. 1 Spot at Family Life Conference", *Journal of Housing* (May 1948): 125.

[7] Fish, *Story of Housing*, 474–75.

way, the subsidies worked in the way intended, and families bought homes that otherwise would not have been built or purchased. [8]

Indeed, by the 1950s, these Americans had entered the golden age of the middle-class welfare state, as the frightening innovations of the New Deal seemed to settle into a comfortable web of federal security: a subsidized home, an insured job paying a family wage, and a modest government old age pension. Mounting prosperity might have posed a ticklish problem for these Americans, as raw consumerism threatened historic American virtues such as modesty and frugality. However, investment in home life provided a solution, as "family-centered spending reassured Americans that affluence would strengthen the American way of life". [9] Nearly the whole increase in the gross national product recorded in the mid-1950s came from spending on appliances, automobiles, and residential construction. [10] The U.S. birthrate climbed from 19.4 per 1,000 persons in 1940 to 25.3 in 1957; the number of children born in the latter year reached 4,300,000. The divorce rate fell steadily through the 1950s, while the creation of new family households soared. Viewed from the perspective of the early 1960s, the government's profamily housing policy could be judged fairly as a dazzling triumph.

At another level, though, federal intrusion into housing markets began to exhibit the more disruptive aspects of centralized social engineering. To begin with, the massive movement of Americans into suburban communities was not solely a response to demand, but rather part of a comprehensive plan to decentralize urban areas for reasons of national defense. A special 1951 issue of the influential *Bulletin of the Atomic Scientists* looked at "Defense through Decentralization: A Symposium

[8] See Harvey S. Rosen, "Owner Occupied Housing and the Federal Income Tax: Estimates and Simulations", *Journal of Urban Economics* 6 (1979): 263–64.

[9] Elaine Tyler May, *Homeward Bound: American Families in the Cold War Era* (New York: Basic Books, 1988), 166.

[10] Ibid., 167.

on Dispersal". While wishing for "world government" as the only long-term solution to the atomic problem, the editors called for the immediate decentralization of the nation's cities and industries as a measure of civil defense. All future residential development, one article stated, should be guided toward suburbs or "garden cities" located in the open countryside. This dispersion of America's population "would so reduce the advantages an enemy might hope to obtain by dropping his supply of bombs that . . . he might decide not to use the weapon at all". Also needed was "speeding up construction of broad express highways through our large cities" to link these dispersed residential and industrial centers together.

It was clear to the authors of a second article that "no private builder" could fulfill these goals and that archaic community sentiments, private property rights, and local political foot dragging also stood in the way. Only a federal urban planning mechanism, armed with the right to condemn and seize needed land and overcome local obstructions, could develop a rational policy toward dispersion. Fortunately, they concluded, the government already had the power through the FHA mortgage and GI insurance programs to push most new construction out to the urban fringe. This power should be fully exercised in line with the national defense "imperative" for "orderly dispersal" of the cities.[11]

The more robust federal agency for central planning of this sort was not secured. However, FHA guidelines did steadily gain a strong suburban bias in the 1950s, while the Interstate Highway Act of 1956 authorized $100 billion for construction of the expressways that would strengthen national security.

At the same time, federal policy goals absorbed prevailing theories from the fields of psychology and family sociology and used them to reshape both the environment and design of

[11] See "The Only Real Defense"; Donald Monson and Astrid Monson, "Program for Urban Dispersal"; and William L. C. Wheaton, "Federal Action toward a National Dispersal Policy", *Bulletin of the Atomic Scientists: A Magazine for Science and Public Affairs* 7 (Sept. 1951): 242–50, 271–75.

new American housing. Toward this end, urban planners strove "to keep alive or to revive . . . a social climate characterized by close internal cohesion among neighbors". Where the *Gemeinschaft* community of the village had failed, they believed that modern urban planning aimed at "community building" could succeed. [12]

Residential architects turned with great interest to studies of the social–psychological effects of housing. A few suggested little impact. Bennett Berger's investigation of a blue-collar tract development outside San Jose, California, found little change among the inhabitants relative to class identification, church attendance, and social participation that derived from the migration to the suburbs. [13] William Dobriner's investigation of suburbia reported similar results. [14]

However, the more eagerly devoured studies showed positive and significant effects of housing environment on human behavior, particularly the strengthening of the nuclear family composed of an employed father, an at-home mother, and their children. Peter Mann reported a "latent neighborliness" in the suburbs that other investigators had missed, representing a modified form of community social integration. [15] Using English samples, J. M. Mogey found that families moving to a suburban housing estate "seemed to have drawn closer together" into nuclear units. Where society in the urban slums rested on external loyalties to social groups, pub life, and extended kin, the suburbs encouraged "the emergence of something like the companionship type of the family". Wives in the

[12] Svend Reimer, "Villagers in Metropolis", *British Journal of Sociology* 2 (1951): 31–33.

[13] Bennett M. Berger, *Working Class Suburbs* (Berkeley and Los Angeles: University of California Press, 1960).

[14] William M. Dobriner, *Class in Suburbia* (Englewood Cliffs, NJ: Prentice-Hall, 1963).

[15] Peter H. Mann, "The Concept of Neighborliness", *American Journal of Sociology* 60 (Sept. 1954): 163, 168.

suburb "spoke much less favorably about a job", while "the conjugal type of family [strove] to discover itself".[16] A similar study of families in Minneapolis found that those moving from slums to a government-planned new community gained significantly more in terms of "social participation" and "social status" than control group families left behind.[17] A comprehensive investigation of black families in Baltimore, Maryland, led by Daniel Wilner, found encouraging evidence that movement from the slums to a federal housing project had positive social results. Children and adults under age 35 recorded marked improvements in their health. The level of common family activities and the mother's discipline of offspring also improved, and the children were more readily promoted in school (even if school test scores showed no significant gains).[18]

Irving Tallman and Ramona Morgner studied blue-collar families in Minneapolis, comparing attitudes of those who had moved to suburbia with a control group that had remained in the slums. On the one hand, they found that the move to the suburbs brought a weakening of bonds to extended family members and old friends. On the other hand, they discovered greater "neighboring" in the suburbs and concluded: "The fact that the suburban families were less apt to evidence close involvement with old friends and relatives and conjugal role segmentation suggests a shift away from the traditional [extended family] . . . and toward a more nuclear type of family organization." The only negative note was found among suburban

[16] J. M. Mogey, "Changes in Family Life Experienced by English Workers Moving from Slums to Housing Estates", *Marriage and Family Living* 17 (May 1955): 123–28.

[17] F. Stuart Chapin, "An Experiment on the Social Effects of Good Housing", *American Sociological Review* 5 (Dec. 1940): 868, 875–77.

[18] Daniel M. Wilner, Rosabelle Price Walkley, Thomas C. Pinkerton, and Matthew Tayback, *The Housing Environment and Family Life: A Longitudinal Study of the Effects of Housing on Morbidity and Mental Health* (Baltimore: Johns Hopkins University Press, 1962), 243–52.

women, whose "forced nuclearization" had resulted in higher levels of loneliness and unease. [19]

Architects and planners gave particular attention to the work of Ernest Rutherford, William Ogburn, Ernest W. Burgess, and Henry J. Locke. Ogburn and Rutherford emphasized that "there is a considerable and increasing disorganization of the family" that would be countered only as the family adjusted to be in line with modern developments. Taking a more optimistic reading of the same situation, Burgess and Locke argued that as the family shed its formal legal and economic functions, it reorganized on the principle of companionship. In the future, they indicated, the "companionship family" would predominate, resting on "the mutual affection, the sympathetic understanding, and the comradeship of its members". As the home became a place for psychological intimacy, democracy, and love, governmental and other external institutions would solidify control over the old family functions of production, education, financial security, child production, and youth training. [20]

Urban planner John Dean drew the conclusion that "it becomes possible . . . to maintain family interaction without recourse to the traditional housekeeping dwelling unit." He believed that units "inherited from the family farm" with a production orientation could be replaced by rational, flexible housing designs more in consonance with modern life patterns focused on consumption. [21] Theorist Svend Reimer stressed how recent attention to "family functions as a guide to residential design" had revolutionized home architecture. "The goal of home construction", he said, "lies in the social dimension:

[19] Irving Tallman and Ramona Morgner, "Lifestyle Differences Among Urban and Suburban Blue-Collar Families", *Social Forces* 48 (March 1970): 334–48.

[20] See Ernest Rutherford Groves and William Ogburn, *American Marriage and Family Relationships* (New York: Henry Holt, 1928), 106, 121; and E. W. Burgess and H. J. Locke, *The Family* (New York: American Book Company, 1945), 651, 654–72.

[21] John P. Dean, "Housing Design and Family Values", *Land Economics* 29 (May 1953): 128–41.

it is a frictionless family life." Reimer added that "housing attitudes must be related to long-term trends of social change in the family." Functional architecture "has promoted a definite way of life and left unmistakable traces on the contemporary housing scene", including the abandonment of formal rooms such as the parlor and single-purpose dining room and of work rooms once devoted to home production, and their replacement by "flexible rooms that serve the everyday life of the family and reduce household chores to the minimum". Reimer urged that much more emphasis be given to "livability studies", which examine "exactly what American families do in the homes", and that homes should be designed and built accordingly.[22]

These functionalist assumptions about the loss of family tasks, the collapse of family production, and the reorganization of the suburban family around its intimate nuclear core worked themselves subtly, yet deeply, into federal housing policy. The official "Fannie Mae" history of housing, for example, stressed that "the family was no longer the basic economic as well as the social unit". Real productive work took place elsewhere. Relative to home design, this meant that "there was no longer so great a need for attics, sheds, storage cellars, work rooms, sewing rooms, etc." Easy access to "processed food supplies" meant less need for pantries and large kitchens. The loss of the family's social role also implied less need for "the drawing rooms and grand staircases of former years". Instead, the new "companionship family" needed "open plans with flexible spaces that could be adapted to the family's more informal lifestyle. . . . Space and facilities for nurturing . . . were needed to replace the space for workshops that had been used when economic function was so important."[23]

FHA guidelines turned this theory into reality. FHA mort-

---

[22] Svend Reimer, "Architecture for Family Living", *Journal of Social Issues* 7 (1951): 140–51.

[23] Fish, *Story of Housing,* 476–78.

gages were systematically denied to any residence that contained facilities designed for use as a productive shop, office, separate apartment for extended family member or renter, or preschool.[24] Other FHA rules discouraged both regional and experimental architectures, favoring instead "conservative" design focused on a few models: Cape Cod, Colonial, the "split level", and the "basic ranch". The agency's *Underwriting Training Handbook* cast both problems under the rubric of conformity and nonconformity, explaining: "The significance of nonconformity in real estate is that as the degree of nonconformity progresses farther from a reasonable degree of conformity with other properties in the neighborhood, the value of the nonconforming property becomes less and less."[25] In sum, housing design for the suburbs would follow assumptions about family function and the demise of the home economy; conformity would be pursued, and favored dwelling forms would supplant the antiquated three-story house of the pre-1933 era.

Federal subsidies, resting on these assumptions, became massive. In 1966, one calculation found that federal tax benefits for home ownership alone were worth $7 billion, roughly 17 percent of the $42 billion of income tax collected from homeowners that year.[26] Another study conducted in 1970 discovered the value of these tax benefits to be roughly $10 billion.[27] Less easily calculated, but very real, were the benefits provided through the FHA, VA, and "Fannie Mae" programs.

For this public price, Americans gained a dramatic expansion

[24] Wright, *Building the Dream,* 247.

[25] Federal Housing Administration, *Underwriting Training Handbook,* vol. 1, pamphlet HH 2.6/6:un 2/2v.1 (1961), 30.

[26] Aaron, *Shelter and Subsidies,* 55.

[27] Michelle J. White and Laurence J. White, "The Tax Subsidy to Owner-Occupied Housing: Who Benefits?" *Journal of Public Economics* 3 (1977): 111. See also Earl R. Rolph, "Discriminatory Effects of the Income-Tax Treatment of Owner-Occupants", *National Tax Journal* 26 (Sept. 1973): 471–82; and David Laidler, "Income Tax Incentives for Owner-Occupied Housing", in *The Taxation of Income from Capital,* ed. Martin J. Bailey and Arnold C. Harberger (Washington, DC: The Brookings Institution, 1969), 50–63.

of the nation's housing stock. Yet they also witnessed a considerable redistribution of income from the poor toward the wealthy. One scholar calculated that a homeowner with a $50,000 income in 1971 received a tax saving equal to one-third of his total housing cost, compared to a mere one-dollar gain for the homeowner with a $3,000 income.[28] In addition, the federally guided housing system produced a startling over-investment in housing, calculated by two reseachers to be 32 percent for those with incomes over $35,000.[29] Third, the system imposed a heavy price penalty on rental units and renters.[30] Finally, as economists frequently stressed, federal incentives retarded other forms of capital investment, helping to cause a net reduction in American productivity growth rates.[31]

If this inefficient allocation of resources had been the only price paid and if family life was demonstrably stronger over the long term, it might have been judged to be worth the sacrifice. However, other costs of federal housing policy—the loss of regional variation in land use and housing design, the intentional abandonment of extended family bonds, the deliberate weakening of the residual family economy, and the consequent isolation and devaluation of the woman in the home—were also imposed, albeit on a deferred basis, beginning in the late 1960s.

At that time, housing advocates believed that the social equations of the 1950s would continue to hold: more young adults would mean more companionship marriages and more children, which in turn would require more suburban housing. As one writer described the situation in 1968: "A huge increase in the number of families was imminent, as children born during the post–World War II baby boom matured, left home, and formed households of their own. Clearly, these new families

[28] Hartman, *Housing and Social Policy,* 109.
[29] White and White, "Tax Subsidy to Owner-Occupied Housing", 123.
[30] Ibid., 126.
[31] See George Sternlieb and James W. Hughes, *America's Housing: Prospects and Problems* (New Brunswick, NJ: Center for Urban Policy Research, Rutgers University, 1980), 89.

would create a housing shortage unless residential construction increased rapidly." [32] President Lyndon Johnson used this scenario to mobilize passage of the Housing and Urban Development Act of 1968, "the most ambitious housing bill in the nation's history". [33] This measure committed the nation to building or rehabilitating 26 million housing units in the 1969–78 decade. Among the provisions, it increased FHA mortgage ceilings, subsidized interest rates for home purchases by persons with low incomes (reducing their real net interest to 1 percent), and established the Government National Mortgage Association ("Ginnie Mae") to buy FHA and other loans at a subsidized or nonmarket rate. The goal of delivering a decent home to every American family finally seemed within the government's grasp.

Yet the housing market was soon behaving in weird and unpredicted ways, as goals and human behavior sharply diverged. The overriding theme of these new developments was dissolution of the basic linkage between family and housing in America.

On the one hand, a massive investment in housing certainly occurred, as residential, nonfarm mortgage debt rose from $358 billion in 1970 to $2.162 trillion in 1987, an absolute increase of 503 percent and an after-inflation increase of 311 percent. On the other hand, a sharply declining proportion of these homes were being purchased by married-couple families. In 1960, families represented 85 percent of all households in distinct dwelling units; by 1989, only 70 percent. Married-couple families, which accounted for 75 percent of all households at the dawn of the 1960s, amounted to only 56 percent by 1989. "Nonfamily households", ranging from single individuals to cohabiting couples to communal arrangements, climbed from 7,895,000 in 1960 to 11,945,000 in 1970 and to a startling 26,994,000 by 1989, a 228 percent increase in less than 30 years.

---

[32] Aaron, *Shelter and Subsidies,* 1.
[33] From Mason, *History of Housing,* 134.

Meanwhile, traditional households steadily declined, both relatively and absolutely. The number of married-couple households in owner-occupied homes, husband aged between 25 and 34 — the implicit target population for the Housing Act of 1968 — actually declined by 2 percent in the 1970–87 period. While the number of one-person households in owner-occupied units soared by 216 percent between 1970 and 1987, the number of five-person households fell 2 percent, and households with six or more persons plunged 51 percent.[34]

In short, an increase in the number of owner-occupied homes, financed by a staggering rise in debt, no longer seemed to be aiding family life. Indeed, after 1968 one could point to a correlation between home purchases and family dissolution. What was happening?

Some commentators speculated that the United States had become the world's first "post shelter" society. Official publications noted that houses were increasingly purchased with "resalability" rather than "livability" in mind and added that there was no longer a "standard family" guiding housing demand.[35] Other analysts noted that "the classic urban housing problem" of providing shelter to large families of limited means was "on the verge of becoming a historical artifact", simply because such families were disappearing. At the same time, housing in America grew much more important as a form of investment and forced savings and as a hedge against inflation, than as a refuge from the elements. This meant that "the 'safe, sound,

[34] Data from U.S. Department of Commerce, Bureau of the Census, *American Housing Survey for the United States in 1987,* H-150-87, tables 2-9, 9-9; U.S. Department of Commerce, Bureau of the Census, *Annual Housing Survey: 1980,* pt. A, H-150-80; U.S. Department of Commerce, Bureau of the Census, *1980 Census of Housing: Metropolitan Housing Characteristics, United States Summary,* HC80-2-1, tables A-10, A-21, A-23; and *Statistical Abstract of the United States, 1990* (Washington, DC: U.S. Government Printing Office, 1990), tables 55, 808.

[35] Fish, *Story of Housing,* 484–85.

sanitary' provisions of a generation ago no longer have relevance to the house search by middle America."[36]

At a more fundamental level, there is evidence to suggest that housing supply was now driving housing demand and that the federally subsidized and managed housing market—initially created to aid family life—was now subsidizing and encouraging family breakup. Throughout this period, for example, expansion of the nation's housing supply continued, while average household size declined. The number of housing units climbed from 53,024,000 in 1960 to 90,888,000 in 1987. Yet in 1960, the average household had 3.33 members; by 1970, 3.14; by 1980, 2.76; and by 1987, only 2.64. Viewed another way, while the population of the United Staes grew by 10.3 million people, or 5 percent in the 1970–76 period, the number of households rose by 9.5 million, nearly 15 percent. This meant, in rough terms, that for every individual added to the population in this period, a new household in a distinct dwelling also formed. Indeed, if households in 1987 had been the same average size as in 1960, the nation would have needed 18.1 million fewer dwellings.[37]

Amazingly, this change reached its apparent peak during a period (1970–85) when real incomes were relatively stagnant (see Table 2). More amazingly, it happened in a period when the ratio of sales price to median income was rising, from 2.37 in 1970 to 3.05 in 1978. A conclusion is that growing federal subsidy alone made this dramatic divergence between housing and family possible.

In their provocative 1980 study of demand for housing, economists George Sternlieb and James Hughes concluded that "the nation's population is diffusing itself into an expanding supply network." Noting that housing demand since the late 1960s had been driven primarily by the shrinkage in average household size, they proceed to a more disturbing conclusion:

[36] Sternlieb and Hughes, *America's Housing,* 100, 156.
[37] See note 34.

Table 2. Gains in Real Income for Median U.S. Family
(constant 1987 dollars)

Year	Income Gain
1960 to 1965	+ $3,492
1965 to 1970	+ $3,821
1970 to 1975	+ $ 90
1975 to 1980	+ $ 26
1980 to 1985	+ $ 306
1985 to 1987	+ $1,551

Source: Statistical Abstract of the United States, 1989, table 721.

"The very decline in the size of household, with its nominal generation of increased demand for housing units, may in turn be a consequence of the availability and costs of housing units generally." While acknowledging a variety of other probable social causes, they comment that the sharp decline in household size "is at least in part also dependent upon the availability of housing units which permit extended family dissolution". [38]

By what mechanism does this happen? There seem to be three possibilities. First, the nation's very success in building homes appears, perversely, to have encouraged family breakup through separation and divorce, as liberalized eligibility standards and direct subsidies eased the costs of creating two households out of one. Second, direct and indirect subsidies may have encouraged home ownership among singles by substituting government help for the economic gains (such as economies of scale) once provided by marriage and family living. Third, the FHA relaxed in the early 1970s the rule that had limited banks to taking only the husband's income into account when setting the maximum size of a mortgage. This rule change may have had an inflationary effect on the general price of housing, giving the two-income family at least a short-term advantage

[38] Sternlieb and Hughes, *America's Housing,* 58–66.

in the bidding contest while steadily driving one–income families out of the market.

Evidence of a direct federal role in these processes can be
seen through the dramatic change in profile of the households
qualifying for FHA mortgages in the latter 1960s and early
1970s. As late as 1966, a hefty 98.6 percent of Section 203 FHA
mortgages for existing homes went to married-couple families,
with the husband as principal earner — i.e., to the classic "traditional family". Unmarried females accounted for only 0.6 of
a percent and unmarried males only 0.7. A decade later (1976),
the proportion of husband-led families had fallen to 70.5 percent, while the proportion of single women and men receiv-
ing government mortgages climbed, respectively, to 8.1 and
10.9 percent. The category "other combinations", also negligible
in 1966, now accounted for 5.9 percent of mortgages. Meanwhile, the number of new FHA mortgages under this section
going to households with dependent children fell from 70.2
percent in 1968 to 51.4 percent in 1976. For those going to
households with three or more children, the fall was even more
dramatic, from 25.3 to 12.4 percent.[39] Similar trends affected
other FHA programs. Under Section 221(d)(2) mortgages, for
example, married couples still accounted for 87.4 percent of
mortgages as late as 1972, but only for 60.4 percent by 1982.[40]

Data collected by the Chicago Title and Trust Company suggest that another aspect of the dynamic change was the mounting economic pressure on all Americans to defer or forego
children. The changed incentives apparently affected both married and single home buyers. In 1989, 86.8 percent of all couples buying their first homes were dual-income households,
compared to only 64 percent in 1977. Also in 1989, a hefty

[39] U.S. Department of Housing and Urban Development, *Series Data Handbook: A Supplement to FHA Trends. Covering Section 203B Home Mortgage Characteristics,* HH 2.24:978/4 suppl. (1978), 29, 33.

[40] U.S. Department of Housing and Urban Development, *FHA Low Cost
Housing Trends, 1-Family Homes,* sec. 221 (d)(3), pamphlets HH 2.26:971/3-983/4
(1978).

23.2 percent of first-time buyers were "never married singles", a dramatic rise from the late 1970s. Among all first-time buyers (and despite the movement of wives into the labor market), monthly mortgage payments took an average of 34.1 percent of family income in 1989, compared to only 23 percent in 1976. At the same time, these new home buyers were a nearly child-less lot. In 1989, the average repeat buyer had only 1.1 children under age 18. Among first-time buyers, the average number of children was but 0.7, a sharp plunge from the 0.9 figure re-corded only one year earlier. Over a mere two-year span (1987 to 1989), the average size of the new-home-buying household plunged from 2.9 to 2.4.[41]

Shifts in income and price patterns appear to have had a dis-proportionately negative effect on single-income couples with children, making it relatively more difficult for them to buy homes. The collapse of the "family wage" ideal in the 1960s, the relative decline in the average wage paid to young adult males, and changes in the eligibility requirements for home loans to the benefit of working couples and singles combined, to the detriment of traditional employed father/at-home mother families. Results may be seen in Table 3, which presents ratios of the median price paid for a single-family dwelling over the median income of married families, 1970 to 1988, comparing couples with wives in the labor market to those with wives as full-time homemakers. Although all categories faced a greater financial strain in acquiring a house during this period, it was families with wives (and usually children) at home who suffered the most, the ratio rising by 64 percent for them for the pur-chase of a new structure (compared to 38 percent for the work-ing couple) and 33 percent for an existing house (compared to 12 percent).

In odd ways, housing experts tacitly acknowledged this shift toward a postfamily order. A highly laudatory 1982 history

[41] *Who's Buying Houses in America . . . Chicago Title's 14th Annual Survey of Recent Home Buyers* (Chicago: Chicago Title and Trust Co., 1990), 1–3, 16–19.

Table 3. Ratio of Median Price Paid for Single-Family
House over Median Annual Family Income (married couples)

| | Wife in Paid Labor Force | | Wife Not in Paid Labor Force | |
	New House	Existing House	New House	Existing House
1970	1.91	1.87	2.52	2.47
1975	2.28	2.05	3.08	2.77
1980	2.40	2.31	3.41	3.98
1985	2.31	2.07	3.43	3.07
1988	2.63	2.09	4.13	3.28
Change, 1970–88	+38%	+12%	+64%	+33%

Source: *Statistical Abstract of the United States,* 1990, tables 732, 1264.

of American housing gave the purpose of the Housing Act of 1949 as providing "a decent home for every American", conveniently dropping the word *family,* which appeared at the end of the original sentence. [42] A conservative critic of housing subsidies noted in 1990 that "non-family and other non-traditional households have emerged partly because they can meet their housing costs", but merely went on to urge greater attention to the housing needs of singles. [43] America's massive housing program had turned on itself, consuming the very social units it was intended to serve; yet few seemed to notice, even fewer to care.

[42] Mason, *History of Housing,* 53.

[43] Carl Horowitz, *Washington's Continuing Fiction: A National Housing Shortage,* Heritage Foundation backgrounder #783 (Aug. 22, 1990), 6–7.

Four

The Religious Possibility

Although some theorists sought to manipulate labor and housing markets to salvage a viable home life, others looked to the power of religious belief. They hoped that doctrine or teachings on marriage and children would give individuals the power to defy the negative pressures set loose by industrialization and "modernity". In doing so, they ran against the grain of expert opinion.

The dominant assumption of the social sciences had been that inherited communal institutions were out of phase with industrialized America and doomed to disappear. Religion and family, the modernists said, were particularly archaic, incompatible with economic, technical, and philosophical changes. William D'Antonio, past president of the Society for the Scientific Study of Religion, summarized a century of opinion, citing the conflict between the "dominant values" of American industrial society — individual achievement, efficiency, progress, faith in science, material comfort, equality, and freedom — and the more communal, self-denying religious virtues of respect for human life, sexual restraint, patriarchy, devotion to family, and love of neighbor. The former values, he said, invariably won out over the latter. In the twentieth century, religion proved unable to sustain convictions that involved personal restraint and so had shifted "away from dogma and unqualified obedience to hierarchy and toward imagery, story, community, and commitment based on love and friendship".[1]

[1] William D'Antonio, "Family Life, Religion, and Society Values and Structures", in *Families and Religions: Conflict and Change in Modern Society,* ed. William V. D'Antonio and Joan Aldous (Newbury Park, CA: Sage, 1983), 81–83, 87, 95–98; and D'Antonio, "The American Catholic Family: Signs of Cohesion and Polarization", *Journal of Marriage and Family* 47 (May 1985): 396.

Others held to an alternate possibility: that numerous Americans might adhere to religiously grounded morality in ways that affected their daily behavior. As sociologist Robert Nisbet once described this possibility, neither science, nor technology, nor the city was "inherently incompatible with the existence of moral values and social relationship which will do for modern man what the extended family, the parish, and the village did for earlier man".[2]

Reviewing the historical record, the Christian and Jewish faiths in America have given witness, at different times and in different ways, to both possibilities. Within the Christian sphere, the Protestant, Catholic, and Mormon communities have each had distinctive teachings on family relationships. Although the former two are much more significant in historical and numerical terms, Mormonism offers a unique bond of dogma to family and an instructive response to modernity. The common story is one of dogmatic surety on the family in the nineteenth century, emergence of religiously disturbing behavior in the early twentieth century, an apparent mid-century revival of religious familism among some religious traditions, and troubled signs after 1960 that belief alone might not be sufficient to the antimodernist, family-sustaining task.

Each major religious group brought to America a distinctive perspective on the family. Although culturally marginal in the United States until after 1900, Jewish rabbinic tradition gave strong emphasis to family living. Jews viewed the divine command "Be fruitful and multiply" (Gen 1:28) as establishing a mitzvah, or obligation, to marry and bear children. Almost alone among the great world religions, Judaism never regarded the renunciation of a normal sex life, marriage, and children as a virtue. Even among the Hasidic ascetics, the greatest importance was assigned to the creation of a normal and responsible marital life. Rabbinical interpretation said that anyone who

---

[2] Quotation from Roy W. Fairchild and John Charles Wynn, *Families in the Church: A Protestant Survey* (New York: Association Press, 1961), 22.

did not contribute to the propagation of the race "is as though he sheds blood and diminishes the Divine Image". Any man "who has no wife is not a complete man". Even study of the Torah should wait until marriage; according to Rab Judah, "A man marries first, and then studies." When the individual faced the Day of Judgment, the question "Did you fulfill your duty with respect to establishing a family?" would certainly be asked.

Concerning sex, the Jew had two obligations: *pru u'rvu*, or procreation, and *onah*, or sexual pleasure. Since the former applied only to men, Jewish women were usually able to use birth control as a regulator of family spacing and size. As Rabbi Moses Schreiber said in 1821: "She is not bound to torment herself on account of her submission to her husband" and "need not destroy [her]self in order to populate the world." At the same time, though, observation of the laws of *niddah* ensured that a couple's sexual contact occurred at the most fertile time of a woman's menstrual cycle, which had a pronatalist intention and effect.[3]

Christian theological understanding of the family, crafted in tension with Judaism and rooted in the Old and New Testaments, took variable forms in the vortex of the Protestant Reformation of the sixteenth century.

Reformer Martin Luther referred to the Old Testament in attacking the monastic orders as unbiblical, and in condemning the clerical ideals of virginity and celibacy for fostering immorality and social irresponsibility. Marriage was not a secondary, inferior state, he said, but rather the highest of estates, "the real religious order on earth", divinely established and "pleasing to God and precious in his sight". Moreover, reproduction was not an option. Rather, God's words in Genesis 1:28, "Be fruitful and multiply", were "a divine ordinance which

---

[3] Useful, if disparate summaries of Jewish conceptions of family life and fertility are found in Abba Hillel Silver, *Where Judaism Differed: An Inquiry into the Distinctiveness of Judaism* (New York: Macmillan, 1956), 190–200; and Susan Weidman Schneider, *Jewish and Female: Choices and Changes in Our Lives Today* (New York: Simon & Schuster, 1984), 225–28, quote on p. 226.

it is not our prerogative to hinder or ignore". Luther praised
the high fertility of the ancient Israelites and wrote that "a
woman is not created to be a virgin, but to conceive and bear
children" and to build homes for Christian nurture. He urged
that they marry early and have as many children as possible,
for "this is the purpose for which they exist."[4]

As the Protestant rebellion matured, a fairly consistent theology of marriage and family emerged. According to the reformers, the blessing of marriage made it possible for mankind
to know, love, and obey God; it subordinated the impulses
toward concupiscence and fornication to natural and legitimate
ends; it stabilized individuals and brought civil peace; and it
imparted to each new generation the values by which society
at large was governed. Although the reformers eliminated marriage from the list of Christian sacraments, they continued to
view it as a spiritual bond superior to all other natural arrangements, and they expected legislators to govern marriage through
biblical (usually meaning Old Testament) principles and to pun-
ish those who offended Christian morality.

This "home-centered" religion, this "school of faith" called
family, came to North America with the Jamestown and Massachusetts colonies in the seventeenth century. Daily family
prayer, Bible reading, and the religious training of children and
servants were central activities for the colonists, with the father
in the role of domestic priest. Although some decay in this family religion was evident by the time of the American War of
Independence,[5] the early nineteenth century witnessed a renewed emphasis on Protestant family life. Visible manifestations
included the quest for a godly architecture. In his *The True Principles of Pointed or Christian Architecture* (1841), A. W. Pugin
described the spiritual and moral impact of Gothic design.[6] The

[4] *Luther's Works,* Vol. 45 (Philadelphia: Muhlenburg Press, 1962), 18, 39–42, 154–55; and Ozment, *When Fathers Ruled,* 1–2, 100–19.

[5] See McDannell, *Christian Home,* 4–5.

[6] Pugin's importance is cited in Kenneth Clark, *The Gothic Revival* (New York: Harper & Row, 1962), 125–26.

use of stained glass and the appearance of iconic Protestant art such as the sampler and furniture such as the parlor organ visibly marked the Protestant American home with these mediating and unifying religious symbols.

Built in suburban or rural areas free from the supposed moral and environmental pollutions of the cities, the institution of the Christian home grew in significance. Civic-minded writers said that only family-based religion could shape the virtuous citizens needed for construction of the "righteous empire" in America. As theologian Horace Bushnell put it, "The house, having a domestic spirit of grace dwelling in it, should become the church of childhood, the table and hearth a holy rite, and life [so take on] an element of saving power."[7]

Among Protestant theologians, two distinct variations of family piety emerged, with gender as the distinguishing fact. "Paternalistic Protestantism" cast the father as king, prophet, and priest. According to Reverend John Power, the family was a "miniature empire" over which the husband and father ruled by divine appointment. The Ladies Depository of 1871 declared that the father served "as priest of the family", the mediator with God who presented a family's prayers to heaven, and so became "the crowning glory of domestic piety and devotion". As prophet, moreover, the father made religious statements and offered biblical interpretations to his family and expected their obedience.[8]

"Maternal Protestantism" found its fullest expression in the influential work of Catharine Beecher. With men irretrievably drawn out of the home into the competitive industrial world,

[7] Horace Bushnell, *Christian Nurture* (New Haven: Yale University Press, 1967), 12 (originally published 1888). Also McDannell, *Christian Home,* 21, 28–48; Fishman, *Bourgeois Utopias,* 121–33; and Benjamin Smith, *Family Religion, or the Domestic Relations as Regulated by Christian Principles* (Philadelphia: Presbyterian Board of Education, 1852), 23.

[8] Quoted in McDannell, *Christian Home,* 109–12; Smith, *Family Religion,* 24–32; and Reverend John H. Power, *Discourse on Domestic Piety and Family Government* (Cincinnati: L. Swarmstedt & A. Poe, 1854), 11–14.

it fell to the Christian mother to serve as God's agent for the religious training of children. Bible readings, hymn singing, prayer, and basic education in the home became the mother's duty in the new world, where work and home life had been radically separated.[9]

All Protestant authors, though, agreed that the primary purposes of "the family constitution" were "the multiplication of mankind" and "the preservation and bodily welfare of our children". They also believed that "happy homes make a happy state" and that the way "to secure national blessings . . . is to secure family blessings".[10] At times, this orientation even tended to elevate the family over the individual as the vehicle for salvation. On the judgment day, said one Methodist writer, "whole families" would stand together on the right hand of God, successful Christian homes that had now been elevated into "the brotherhood of heaven".[11]

The shock of the Protestant rebellion forced Roman Catholicism into a reconsideration of some elements of its understanding of family, particularly of the canon law concept of "secret marriage" which had become an object of frequent abuse.[12] Central Catholic doctrines, though, were eventually reaffirmed: the spiritual primacy of holy vows, the monastic life, and celibacy; the sacramental, indissoluable nature of marriage; the role of the church and its priesthood as the mediators between God and man and the only channel for salvation; and an implicit pronatalism.

Theological developments in the nineteenth century intensified Catholic consideration of the family. Proclamation of the dogma of the Immaculate Conception in 1854 was followed within four years by reported appearances of the Virgin Mary in Lourdes and in 1879 of Mary, Saint Joseph, and Saint John

[9] Beecher and Stowe, *American Woman's Home,* chap. 1; and McDannell, 47, 115, 128–36.

[10] Smith, *Family Religion,* 30–31, 177.

[11] Power, *Discourse on Domestic Piety,* 179–84.

[12] Ozment, *When Fathers Ruled,* 25–27.

in County Mayo, Ireland. Devotion to Mary and the use of the rosary increased during this period, particularly among women who empathized with the healing and nurturing roles of the Blessed Mother. In the encyclical *Fidentem piumque animum* (1896), Pope Leo XIII urged whole families to say the rosary together, which represented a new form of home-centered Catholic activity. *Quamquam pluries* (1889) enhanced devotion to Saint Joseph, and in 1893, Leo designated special indulgences for those who prayed before the image of the Holy Family.[13]

Papal pronouncements on the role of the family in society, noted earlier, also made their initial appearance. In a series of encyclicals, Leo XIII tied more closely the health of the family to the safety of the modern world. He affirmed "the natural and primeval right of marriage" and "the society of the household" as the proper foundations for social and economic theory in the new, industrializing age.[14] Although the Church did not establish an ideal family size, large families were viewed as signs of fidelity to Church doctrines prohibiting the restriction of births and were praised from the pulpit and in print. By way of contrast, small families or childlessness were labeled as "sad", "incomplete", or "tragic".

Mid-nineteenth-century Catholic writers in America embraced these themes, labeling the family "the nursery of the nation" and the source of virtuous citizens. Home, they said, was a sample of "the joys of Heaven", "the spot where angels find a resting place", a "sweet image of God's home on high". Monsignor Maurice de Hulst saw the family replicating the Trinity: "The majesty of the heavenly Father has descended upon the head of the family circle; the beauty of the mother is illuminated by the splendor of the Son; and love, the work of the Holy Spirit, unites the father and mother, and brings forth the

---

[13] See McDannell, *Christian Home*, 13–16.

[14] Pope Leo XIII, *Rerum Novarum*, in *Two Basic Social Encyclicals* (Washington, DC: The Catholic University of America Press, 1943), 5–11.

fruit that will cement their union." The Catholic mother became a "home hero", a woman "cloistered in her home", a
"priestess of the domestic shrine" who "cultivates religion
in her family and instructs her children in its truths". Private chapels, oratories, and religious lithographs also found
their way into Catholic homes. Some enthusiastic Catholic
writers passed beyond the bounds of orthodoxy and elevated
the family above the Church, seeing the former as a vehicle
effecting salvation and the latter as a structure primarily designed "to secure the existence, the honor, and the happiness
of every home".[15]

Mormonism, born in the 1830s through the prophecies
of Joseph Smith, offers a revealing counterpoint to the dominant Protestant and Catholic faiths in America. Its identity
with polygamy in the nineteenth century and with the large
family after 1900 has obscured the consistent aspects of Mormon family doctrine: the condemnation of sexual intercourse
outside marriage; encouragement of universal marriage at a
young age; expected high fertility; male leadership in the church
and home, modeled on Old Testament patriarchs; the definition of a woman's role as that of mother and homemaker;
strong endorsement of the home as a center for economic activities such as gardening, canning, and sewing; and sanctions
against divorce.

More broadly, though, the Mormon religion was not just
concerned with the family: "In the last analysis it really is *about*
the family."[16] In the emerging Mormon theology, men and
women attained the highest degree of salvation through "eternal marriage" or "sealing", a dispensation by the church that
guaranteed to a couple marriage in the next life if they remained
faithful. Like the Protestants, Mormons gave particular empha-

[15] McDannell, *Christian Home,* 56–58, 66, 75, 137–40; and Maurice Lesage
d'Hautecoeur d'Hulst, *The Christian Family: Seven Conferences,* trans. Bertrand
L. Conway (New York: J. F. Wagner, 1905), 9.

[16] Lawrence Foster, "Between Heaven and Earth", *Sunstone* 7 (1982): 7.

sis to the words of Genesis 1:28 – "Be fruitful and multiply" –
yet within a decidedly different context: God should be viewed
as literally an eternal father who once lived in a mortal state,
married, proved faithful, and now procreated spirit children.
All those now living were literally the offspring of God, spirit
children given flesh on earth. Countless more waited to be
born, and merit went to those believers who bore many children. Moreover, Mormons believed that "as God is, man may
become"; that this life was the time to prepare both to meet
the God of this world and to become a god, procreating still
more spirit children for other worlds. Accordingly, Mormon
doctrine held "an overwhelming emphasis on fertility, not only
mortal, but pre-mortal and post-mortal as well".[17]

During the late nineteenth century, as the polygamy question pitted the Latter-day Saints against the U.S. government,
church leaders held firm: attacks against polygamous marriage
and arguments favoring fertility limitation were seen as related
assaults on the basic Mormon tenets of marriage and parenthood. With the official abandonment of polygamy in the 1890s,
the nuclear family was embraced in its stead. Yet the emphasis
on fertility remained. As church leader Heber J. Grant com-
mented in 1913: "I am thankful that healthy, vigorous, strong,
sweet babies are the best crop of Utah, and I hope and pray
earnestly that it will ever be so. I hope that the fashion which
is a thousand times worse than the fashions of dress, namely,
that of drying up the fountains of life, will never become popular among the Latter-day Saints."[18]

In the decades either side of 1900, though, a time of troubles

---

[17] Donald W. Hastings, Charles R. Reynolds, and Ray R. Canning, "Mor-
monism and Birth Planning: The Discrepancy between Church Authorities'
Teachings and Lay Attitudes", *Population Studies* 26, no. 1 (1972): 22; and James
E. Smith, "A Familistic Religion in a Modern Society", in *Contemporary Mar-
riage: Comparative Perspectives on a Changing Institution,* ed. Kingsley Davis (New
York: Russell Sage Foundation, 1985), 276–79.

[18] Quoted in Hastings et al., "Mormonism and Birth Planning", 23.

began for defenders of the family shrine in America. The accelerating forces of urbanization, industrialization, and ethnic assimilation and philosophical challenges such as feminism, Darwinism, scientific socialism, and neo-Malthusianism seemed to shake the foundation of belief and of the familial behavior that it sustained.

Among American Jews, it is true that guiding rabbinic principles did not substantially change. Behavior, though, did. After 1900, the general trend was a steady erosion in fertility, with the predictable exceptions of the Orthodox and (after 1939) the Hasidim. Although exceeding the fertility of both whites and blacks without religion, Jews as a whole have consistently shown the lowest fertility of all American religious groups. The comprehensive 1973 and 1976 National Surveys of Family Growth, for example, showed that married Jewish women ages 15 through 44 then had an average of 1.86 children and expected an average of 2.25, considerably below both Catholic and Protestant figures. Michael Yoder reported in 1980 that Jews actually showed a unique negative relationship between religiosity and desired fertility: the more active they were in religious matters, the fewer children they wanted. Another survey suggested why. Although finding that young Jewish women were more likely to be married than their Catholic counterparts, the former also were better educated, were more vocal feminists, and had more closely tied their self-esteem to their careers rather than to their marriages.

The contrast with Jews residing in Israel was startling. In general, Israeli fertility was significantly higher: in 1975, the average Jewish woman under age 45 had 2.83 children, compared to the 1.86 figure for her American counterpart. Several surveys revealed a strong positive correlation between religious observance and family size: the least religious Israeli Jewish women had an average of 1.39 children; those of moderate religiosity, 2.62; and those of high religious activity, 4.48. Contraceptive use, moreover, played no role in this: the differences in degree of usage among the religious categories were not significant.[19]

It appears that in Israel family size operated as a Jewish issue. As Jewish community activist Elaine Shizgal Cohen of Teaneck, N.J., remarked: "There's a joyful acceptance of children in the general culture . . . a widely shared commitment to nation building, unspoken anxieties about the possibility of losing a child to war or terrorism, a post-Holocaust affirmation of Jewish destiny." This same woman described her decision to have a third child as "an act of affirmation and of conscience after the Holocaust and in an age of widespread assimilation". Such attitudes, however, failed to make a statistical dent in America, where the Jewish community faced continued demographic decline. By the 1980s, the New York–based Task Force on Jewish Population, articles on the "Coming Shrinkage of American Jewry", and numerous sermons on fertility within North American synagogues were signs of trouble.[20]

For American Protestants, the spread of liberal theology foreshadowed the decay of family piety in the early twentieth century. Historical criticism of the Bible and doubts about the relevance of doctrine to a scientific industrial age spread in the seminaries. For a time, the atmosphere was frantic, as religious writers sought to reconcile modernist beliefs with old convictions. George Walter Fiske of Oberlin College reflected an almost schizophrenic split on these issues in his 1929 book *The Christian Family*. He welcomed the end of "paternal tyranny", the new freedom which women had won, and the "progress" it all "spells . . . for the race". Yet he quickly descended into a lament over the "rampant individualism" that had "killed the

[19] Shoshana Neuman and Adrian Ziderman, "How Does Fertility Relate to Religiosity: Survey Evidence from Israel", *Sociology and Social Research* 70 (Jan. 1986): 178–80. See also Michael Lee Yoder, "Religion as a Determinant of Fertility among White Americans, 1965", doctoral dissertation (Madison: University of Wisconsin, 1980), 251.

[20] See Schneider, *Jewish and Female,* 371–82; quote p. 382.

old family spirit", the "moral laxity", the rapid increase in divorce, "thrill chasing", and female indulgence in masculine vices. He celebrated female wage earners, yet blamed them for a reduced birthrate, a higher infant mortality rate, increased juvenile delinquency, and the undermining of male wages. "Thank God", he concluded, "the majority of our homes in America are still normal"; yet he dizzily wondered for how much longer.[21]

By the 1930s, though, these laments had ceased, and Protestant emphasis was on adjusting dogma on family and sexuality to meet the new age. The major symbolic event signaling Protestant doctrinal retreat was the 1930 Lambeth Conference, at which the Anglican church overturned its historic opposition to the use of birth control. Not to be outdone, the Committee on Marriage and Home of the Federal Council of Churches issued a statement the next year approving contraception. Both documents emphasized the need to compromise with changing realities.

Sociology and its practitioners also won a new position as interpreters of the modern Christian family. Ernest R. Groves' *Christianity and the Family* (1942) was the religious complement to his influential books chronicling the family's progressive "loss of function". The family, he said, could be regarded as an ally of Christianity. Yet the clear reality of family weakness meant that a new form of guidance from the church was needed, starting "with the presumption that any home deserves strengthening". The Christian family was not an absolute, nor was fidelity: specialists might need to take children away from parents while "the separation of the spouses may also be indicated for the good of one or both." Indeed, the newly therapeutic church should recognize that the "mere keeping of vows" was "a feeble accomplishment" and that it should never insist on "a stereotyped standard of family". Moreover, human need could not be fulfilled these days through the antique family functions of economic sustenance, sex, and childbearing. Rather, Groves said, avoidance of guilt and training in the search for "new spiritual impulses" were the modern Christian imperatives.[22]

Pastoral tracts on the Christian family showed clear signs of degeneration in this era. Stirring endorsements of "the family state" gave way to more cautious descriptions of the family as teacher and useful adjuster of personality and to grave warnings that a stereotyped family form should not be forced on unwilling Christians.[23]

Nonetheless, the "baby boom" of the post–World War II decades swept over the mainline Protestant churches, stimulating a heady hubris about the success of the Christian family. Following the grim days of depression and war, church membership rolls climbed sharply, and nurseries and Sunday schools overflowed with children. Even the Federal Council of Churches (FCC) caught the new spirit, explaining in a 1946 policy statement that "[f]or the individual family, there is nothing more satisfying, even though it may involve real sacrifice, than to have at least three or four children." Popular writers also produced new tracts on the family, echoing those of the nineteenth century. C. R. McBride, for example, saw "the Christian home" as of highest importance to the development of the human race, described marriage without children as "an unnatural thing", and celebrated large families. In *Beautiful Homemaking,* beauty queen and pastor's wife Charlene Johnson affirmed the housewife's position "as just about the most challenging in the world". The husband was, through God's will, "the king of your home". Woman's duty was "to keep Dad at the head of the house",

[22] Ernest R. Groves, *Christianity and the Family* (New York: Macmillan, 1942), 4, 106–11.

[23] See Lewis Joseph Sherrill, *Family and Church* (New York: Abingdon Press, 1937), 72–73, 85–86; *The Family and Its Christian Fulfillment* (New York: Foreign Missions Conference of North America, 1945); and Thomas van Braam Barrett, *The Christian Family* (New York: Morehouse-Gorham, 1958), 69–70.

to shape "a home paradise". Children were "Jesus' little lambs", entrusted to a mother's care, so that "your home can be a little bit of heaven right here on earth". [24]

The 1950s, in short, witnessed an apparent revival of Protestant family piety. It rested, however, on an insecure foundation. In a scathing critique of Protestantism's renewed family centeredness, sociologist Peter Berger argued that social class, economic, and historical factors lay behind the surge in family living, not religious renewal: "It is not a particular family that produces certain political or economic development, but the other way around." Research into the motivation for joining churches showed that new suburban members of the 1950s rarely claimed a life crisis, a conversion experience, or renewed religious sentiments. Rather, "for most of these people the decision to join was prompted by the prospect or presence of children in the family." Church membership was simply another step in constructing the "O.K. world" of the American middle class. [25]

Indeed, by the early 1960s, Protestant intellectual leaders were becoming decidedly hostile to the Christian nuclear family. Marriage and family life were, at best, of secondary importance in the New Testament, they said. The "patriarchal, one-job family", which churches clung to nostalgically, was heading toward the historical ash can. Church structures oppressed women. Christian emphasis on the family was "a new idolatry". It was an error to take Jesus' statements about the

[24] FCC quotation in C. Gregg Singer, *The Unholy Alliance* (New Rochelle, NY: Arlington House, 1975), 179; C. R. McBride, *The Christian Home in a Rural Setting* (Philadelphia: Judson Press, 1953), 7-10, 27-28; and Charlene Johnson, *Beautiful Homemaking* (Rock Island, IL: Augustana Book Concern, 1961), 13-14, 49-53, 59, 73.

[25] Peter Berger, *The Noise of Solemn Assemblies* (New York: Doubleday, 1961), 93ff.; Dennison Nash and Peter Berger, "The Child, the Family, and the 'Religious Revival' of Suburbia", *Journal for the Scientific Study of Religion* 2 (Fall 1962): 85-93; and Gerhard Lenski, *The Religious Factor: A Sociologist's Inquiry* (New York: Doubleday, 1961), 219-22, 226.

family as law. Protestant questioning of the family was "a sign of health".[26]

Ecumenical Protestant bodies reflected this change in emphasis. The World Council of Churches (WCC) focused particularly on the issue of mothers' employment outside the home and finally bowed to "social change", the "fulfillment of personal life", and "personal growth" as the governing moral imperatives. The churches must be change agents, WCC assemblies maintained, and help transform antiquated gender roles into a new egalitarianism on the Scandinavian model.[27]

The National Council of the Churches of Christ went much further, dismissing the historic Christian experience, consciously abandoning biblical family norms, and casting itself into the arms of modern sexology and therapeutic psychology. Its 1961 publication *Foundations for Christian Family Policy* can only be labeled extraordinary. As the proceedings of a conference held earlier in the year, it chronicles the total collapse of the Protestant family ethic. Setting the theme, keynote speaker J. C. Wynn of Colgate Divinity School dismissed existing church pronouncements and books on the family as "depressingly platitudinous", "comfortably dull", and a regretable "works righteousness". A second keynote speaker celebrated the conference as representing the merger of Christianity with the findings of social and medical science, "a mighty symbol of the readiness of the churches . . . to ground their policy formation in objective, solid data".

[26] See Fairchild and Wynn, *Families in the Church,* 15–17, 71–75; Roger Crook, *The Changing American Family* (St. Louis: Bethany Press, 1960), 30–36; and Wallace Denton, *What's Happening to Our Families?* (Philadelphia: Westminster Press, 1963), 204–11.

[27] Department on Cooperation of Men and Women in Church, Family, and Society, World Council of Churches, *Report: Consultation,* held at Cité Universitaire, Paris, France, July 25–30, 1963 (Geneva: World Council of Churches, 1963), sec. III; and *Consultation on Developing Relations of Men, Women, and Children in Our Changing World (with special reference to developments in the Scandinavian societies),* held at St. Katharinastiftelsen, Oskerskar, Sweden, June 28–July 2, 1968 (Geneva: World Council of Churches, 1968), 29–31.

The list of speakers was astonishing, a veritable "Who's Who" of antireligious intellectual celebrities. Lester Kirkendall said that America had now "entered a sexual economy of abundance", a period of unrestrained experimentation in sensual delights, meaning that traditional sexual virtues were irrelevant. Wardell Pomeroy, director of field research for the Institute for Sex Research, explained how the science of sexology demanded the abandonment of moral judgments. He emphasized that "the concept of normality and abnormality is worse than useless. It gets in the way in our thinking." Psychologist Evelyn Hooker described the healthy, well-adjusted lives of most homosexuals and the naturalness of their sexual acts. Planned Parenthood's Mary Calderone urged churches to help individuals shape their own private values about sex, while Alan Guttmacher traced America's mean-spirited abortion policy to the pronatalism of the Jews.

The conference's final report cited "the freedom we have been given in Christ" as justification for movement into a new morality. A different Christian ethic on sexual behavior that was "relevant to our culture" must be developed, one located in the context of scientific discoveries. "Out-dated moralisms" and "respectable traditions" ought to be discarded and marriage should be unmasked as "idolatry".[28]

Later Protestant theological excursions into the family proceeded largely in the same spirit. In a subsequent book, Wynn saw the "isolated nuclear family of today" as "all but powerless", and churches incapable of upholding standards that deviated from actual practice. Herbert Anderson argued that "the privatization of the family can only lead to an emotional incest", while the nuclear family was in "moral bankruptcy".

[28] Elizabeth Stell Genne and William Henry Genne, eds., *Foundations for Christian Family Policy: The Proceedings of the North American Conference on Church and Family, April 30–May 5, 1961* (New York: National Council of the Churches of Christ in the U.S.A., 1961), 19–21, 35–40, 84–85, 92–93, 157–63, 172–73, 197–99, 227, 233, 250–60.

Another theologian argued that there is, as such, no Christian social order. Rather, Christian ethics presupposed "a creative freedom" in which "the inbreaking of the new age into the old is . . . witnessed by the fact of questioning", particularly of the need for marriage.[29]

Official denominational pronouncements showed the same drift, although the pressures of lay opinion sometimes forced a slower pace. Endorsement of abortion rights and the Equal Rights Amendment was almost universal. The Episcopalians, moreover, proclaimed that "our basic assumptions about the family need re-examination." In a 1977 statement, the United Church of Christ urged more favorable attention to "non traditional" living arrangements. In its 1980 Book of Discipline, the United Methodist Church said that the family must encompass "a wider range of options" than the nuclear family. The Lutheran Church in America, in a 1970 statement, seemed primarily intent on warning that "the family should not become centered on itself" and established "a right" not to have children. At the fringe, the Unitarian-Universalist Association urged congregations to provide structured relationships that could "replace family units".[30]

American Catholics in the 1900–40 period behaved increasingly like their Protestant neighbors, at least relative to fertility. Although not conclusive, there were mounting data that suggested a convergence of Protestant and Catholic birthrates in America, a sign of the growing victory of social and economic pressures over the differential influence of belief. At the doctrinal level, there was a sharp contrast with Protestant decla-

[29] J. C. Wynn, *Family Therapy in Pastoral Ministry* (San Francisco: Harper & Row, 1982), 8–9, 11; Herbert Anderson, *The Family and Pastoral Care* (Philadelphia: Fortress Press, 1984), 47–52, 69–76; and Bjorn Bjornsson, *The Lutheran Doctrine of Marriage in Modern Icelandic Society* (Oslo: Universitets förlaget, 1971), 214–22.

[30] Summarized in Barbara Hargrove, "Family in the White American Protestant Experience", in D'Antonio and Aldous, *Families and Religions,* 120–33.

rations, as the church hierarchy labored to shore up orthodoxy on family-related questions. Pius XI issued *Casti connubii* in 1933, which reaffirmed historic Catholic teachings: procreation and the rearing of children as the primary purposes of marriage; marriage as an indissoluble sacrament; limitation of family size only for licit reasons; periodic abstinence as the only licit means of birth control; total abstinence from sexual activity as the rule for the unmarried; and the married woman serving in the home as wife and mother.

In some ways, in fact, the Catholic emphasis on family life was extended. For example, the large Catholic family received explicit theological affirmation in the post–World War II period. As Pope Pius XII declared: "Large families are most blest by God and specially loved and prized by the Church as its most precious treasures. . . . Where you find families of great numbers, they point to: the physical and moral health of a Christian people; a living faith in God and trust in His Providence: the fruitful and joyous holiness of Catholic marriage."[31]

Witnessing, it seems, to this steadfastness in doctrine, the 1945–65 era produced an extraordinary, indeed "heroic", flowering of Catholic family life in America. Although fertility rose for all American religious groups during this period, it rose far more rapidly and continued longer among Catholics. Indeed, there were signs that the American "baby boom" was largely a Catholic phenomenon. The total marital fertility rate for non-Catholics averaged 3.15 children per woman in 1951–55 and 3.14 in 1961–65; for Catholics, the respective figures were 3.54 and 4.25. More dramatic was the return of the large Catholic family: in a survey conducted in 1952–55, only 10 percent of Catholics under age 40 reported having four or more children, a figure close to the 9 percent for Protestants. By

[31] Gabriel Marcel, *Homo Viator,* quoted in Judith Blake, "Catholicism and Fertility: On Attitudes of Young Americans", *Population and Development Review* 10 (June 1984): 32; and Pius XII, "The Large Family Address to the Associations of Large Families of Rome and Italy, Jan. 19, 1958", *The Pope Speaks* 4 (Spring 1958): 363–64.

1957–59, the Protestant figure was unchanged, but the proportion for Catholics had shot up to 22 percent.

Still more surprising was the nature of this postwar resurgence in Catholic fertility. It flourished among the best educated: Catholic women who had attended college were bearing more children than Catholic women without a high school degree. Increased fertility was also found primarily among younger parents: through 1965, each new cohort of parents was more pronatalist in its attitudes than the group before. And it had a clear religious focus: more frequent attendance at Mass was related to more births. Moreover, the rise in fertility was part of a broad commitment to family life, and surveys repeatedly showed Catholic extended-family bonds to be more durable and enjoyment of the parenting task more intense than among non-Catholics. Indeed, the Catholic family ethic, resting on devotion to church teachings, seemed to be reaching new highs in the mid-1960s. Among the American laity, at least, there was no apparent crisis of faith.[32]

Within ten years, though, all of these qualities appeared to have collapsed, utterly and completely, prompting a spate of articles on "the end of Catholic fertility". There is little doubt that the currents of ideas affecting Catholicism in the 1960s — challenges to traditional practices and hierarchical authority in the wake of Vatican II, the Papal encouragement of debate on the contraceptive question in the mid-1960s, followed by the stunning reaffirmation of orthodoxy in *Humanae vitae* (1968), and the impact of feminist and neo-Malthusian tenets on key Catholic elites — lay partly behind this shift. Dissent became legitimized, and doctrinal uncertainty grew. Given the new divisions among theologians and church leaders, it appears that

[32] See William D. Mosher, David P. Johnson, and Majorie C. Horn, "Religion and Fertility in the United States: The Importance of Marriage Patterns and Hispanic Origin", *Demography* 23 (Aug. 1986): 367–69; Blake, "Catholicism and Fertility", 39–40; Lenski, *Religious Factor,* 203, 215–18; and Lincoln H. Day, "Natality and Ethnocentrism: Some Relationships Suggested by an Analysis of Catholic-Protestant Differentials", *Population Studies* 22 (1968): 27–30.

the laity may simply have followed the easiest of several disputed paths of obedience. [33]

Indeed, changes in lay Catholic attitudes and behavior concerning the family have been traced to the specific years 1967–71. In their study of Catholic fertility in Rhode Island, Leon Bouvier and S. L. N. Rao found that average expected family size among Catholics fell from 3.3 children to 2.8 in that period, a substantially greater decline than seen among Protestants. This fall in expected fertility was sharpest for the better educated: among Catholic women with some college education, the decline was from 3.7 to 2.7 children. Moreover, frequency of communion no longer proved to be related to fertility. Even the large family ideal vanished: in 1967, 28 percent of "devout" Catholics planned to have five or more children; by 1971, less than 7 percent did. [34]

Although sociologist Andrew M. Greeley could still identify some distinctive traits of Catholic family life by the mid-1970s, these were of generally diminishing intensity and seemed related more to ethnic past than to doctrine. [35] With only a few and steadily diminishing exceptions, the attitudes of American Catholics could no longer be distinguished from those of Protestants on questions of marriage, divorce, birth control,

[33] See Charles F. Westoff and Elise T. Jones, "The End of 'Catholic' Fertility", *Demography* 16 (May 1979): 209–11; Gerhard Lenski, "The Religious Factor in Detroit: Revisited", *American Sociological Review* 36 (1971): 48–50; Mary Daly, "After the Death of God the Father: Women's Liberation and the Transformation of Christian Consciousness", *Commonweal* (Mar. 12, 1971); reprinted in Carol P. Christ and Judith Plaskow, *Womanspirit Rising* (New York: Harper & Row, 1976), 53–62; and *Humanae Vitae,* trans. M. A. Caligari (Cincinnati, OH: Couple to Couple League, 1983).

[34] Leon Bouvier and S. L. N. Rao, *Socio-religious Factors in Fertility Decline* (Cambridge, MA: Ballinger, 1975), 1–4, 84–91, 156, 158; Charles Westoff and Larry Bumpass, "The Revolution in Birth Control Practices of U.S. Roman Catholics", *Science* 179 (Jan. 12, 1973): 41–44; Andrew Greeley, *The American Catholic: A Social Portrait* (New York: Basic Books, 1977), 189; and Charles F. Westoff and Elise T. Jones, "The Secularization of U.S. Catholic Birth Control Practices", *Family Planning Perspectives* 9 (Sept.-Oct. 1977): 203–7.

[35] Greeley, *American Catholic,* 188–91, 194, 206.

family size, or abortion. Over time, Church actions appeared to complement this drift. The number of marriage annulments, for example, climbed from 338 in 1968 to 52,000 in 1983.

Mormons showed no dramatic deviations in family behavior between 1900 and 1970. In general, they followed the same patterns seen among Protestant Americans: fertility declined in 1900–45, increased between 1945 and 1960, and declined after 1960. Although Mormon fertility over couples' reproductive lifespans was consistently higher throughout these cycles, the difference between Mormons and non-Mormons was steadily diminishing, witnessed by the fall in the ratio of the Mormon/U.S. crude birthrate from 1.60 in 1920 to 1.46 in 1960. The Latter-day Saints had no official position on birth control, and its use by mid-century was widespread. There was every reason to assume that this turn to the rationalized control of child spacing would progressively extend to other areas of life. As Mormon assimilation into American society continued, most sociologists anticipated that "Mormon fertility" would also disappear as a distinctive phenomenon. [36]

In the 1970s and 1980s, though, the general relationship between religion and family grew more complicated. Researchers discovered and emphasized that there were different kinds of Protestants. Although mainline churches remained in theological and numerical tailspins, the fundamentalist churches showed a more vital family religion. At the doctrinal level, the Southern Baptist Convention strengthened in 1981 its affirmation of the patriarchal nuclear family, saying that "the family has been clearly defined in God's Word and accepted by the Jewish and Christian society of America for over two hundred years." [37] Attention also returned to studies that documented a distinctive fundamentalist pronatalism. One investigation, for

[36] Hastings et al., "Mormonism and Birth Planning", 25–29; and Arland Thornton, "Religion and Fertility: The Case of Mormonism", *Journal of Marriage and Family* 41 (Feb. 1979): 134–39.

[37] Reported in Hargrove, "Family in White American Protestant Experience", 135.

example, showed the average ideal family size of southern fundamentalists to be significantly higher (3.4 children) than that of nonfundamentalists (2.8), a difference that held even after controlling for socioeconomic status.[38] Similarly, a 1980 study found "conservative Protestants" to have larger families than "liberal Protestants", with an antiabortion attitude serving as the strongest predictor of desired fertility.[39]

There is also some evidence suggesting that "Catholic fertility" had some resilience into the 1980s. Judith Blake reported in 1984 that the difference between non-Catholic and Catholic family size expectations still existed among high school students and that these expectations were related to degree of religious involvement. In another article, two scholars showed that a significant Catholic-Protestant difference in marital fertility remained (about 0.4 more children per Catholic woman) and that this difference was related to frequency of communion. Others discovered that Catholics remained more likely to have an earlier second birth and that this accelerated pace of fertility was linked to prior attendance at Catholic schools.[40]

True, the meaning of these discoveries was disputed. Sociologist William Mosher argued that the return of Catholic fertility was due solely to the heavy immigration of Hispanic Catholics, whose fertility was 40 percent above that of other U.S. women. Yet the work of others suggested a more complex dynamic. For instance, Nan Johnson found that although Catholics married later than Protestants, they still bore more children and had a higher expected fertility over their reproduc-

---

[38] Gordon F. De Jong, "Religious Fundamentalism, Socio-Economic Status, and Fertility Attitudes in the Southern Appalachians", *Demography* 2 (1965): 540–49.

[39] Yoder, "Religion as a Determinant of Fertility", 230–35.

[40] Blake, "Catholicism and Fertility", 330–32; William D. Mosher and Gerry E. Hendershot, "Religious Factors in the Timing of Second Births", *Journal of Marriage and the Family* 47 (May 1985): 364–65.

tive lifespans. Moreover, attendance at Catholic colleges accounted for almost all of this pronatalist effect. [41]

In the 1970s, moreover, Mormons offered a second instance of religious defiance of contemporary times. Although the U.S. fertility rate of whites continued its post-1960 decline, Utah's fertility actually climbed to a figure nearly twice as high as the national rate.

There was evidence, moreover, that linked this increase to Mormon religious belief. Frequency of attendance at services, the observance of daily worship activities within the family, and the frequency of prayer at home were all positively related to Mormon family size. Doctrinal views on premarital sex had an almost astonishing impact on the sexual behavior of youth. A 1978 survey found that 88 percent of male and 91 percent of female Mormon college students disapproved of premarital sex, compared to 20 percent of male and 38 percent of female non-Mormons. Other investigations showed that the surge in Mormon fertility after 1970 was not due to avoidance of contraceptives (Mormons use birth control at least as often as other Americans), nor to the oppression of women (both Mormon men and women score relatively high on measurements of attitudes about equality). It simply appeared that dogma still mattered. As sociologist James Smith concluded: "Mormons have constructed a temple-centered culture in the midst of modern society where all activities are interpreted in the context of the ultimate Mormon goal of preserving the family into eternity." More impressionistic evidence suggested that the Mormon emphasis on self-sufficiency and home production (including the year's supply of stored food in every home) also played a role in preserving family integrity. [42]

[41] Mosher et al., "Religion and Fertility", 367–79; and Nan Johnson, "Religious Differentials in Reproduction: The Effects of Sectarian Education", *Demography* 19 (Nov. 1982): 495–508.

[42] Smith, "Familistic Religion", 291, 296. See also Michael B. Toney, Banu Golesorkhi, and William F. Stinner, "Residence Exposure and Fertility Expec-

The 1980s, though, brought a more sobering reality. Utah's crude birth rate, which had climbed from 25.5 in 1970 (39 percent above the national average) to 28.6 in 1980 (80 percent above the national figure), fell back to 21.0 in 1987 (only 34 percent above the national figure). The state's marriage rate also became less exceptional, falling from 11.6 in 1980 (9 percent above the national average) to 9.8 in 1988 (1 percent above the U.S. figure). Since about 30 percent of the state's population is non-Mormon, figures for Utah are an imperfect measure of Mormon behavior. Nonetheless, these sharp changes do suggest a distinctive defiance of national norms in the 1970s, followed by a new convergence of Mormons toward national norms in the 1980s. Not coincidentally, church leaders repeatedly warned female members about the distractions of a career, but apparently to little effect. In 1984, 54.41 percent of Utah women were in the paid labor force (1.49 percent *above* the national average). By 1988, the figure was 59.4 percent (4.95 percent *above* the U.S. average). [43]

Looking over the whole century, the lessons of the religious possibility are threefold. To begin with, modern religious belief has a significant, albeit limited, ability to encourage marriage and children. Except among liberal Jews, religiously observant Americans had and continue to have somewhat more stable and larger families than their nonreligious counterparts. [44]

---

tations of Young Mormon and Non-Mormon Women in Utah", *Journal of Marriage and the Family* 47 (May 985): 459–65; Tim Heaton and Sadra Calkins, "Family Size and Contraceptive Use among Mormons, 1965–75", *Review of Religious Research* 25 (Dec. 1983): 102–13; and Moshe Hartman and Harriet Hartman, "Sex Role Attitudes of Mormons vs. Non-Mormons in Utah", *Journal of Marriage and the Family* 45 (Nov. 1983): 897–902.

[43] Data from *Statistical Abstract of the United States,* 1986, 1989, 1990 editions.

[44] See Norval D. Glenn, "The Social and Demographic Correlates of Divorce and Separation in the United States: An Update and Reconsideration", *Journal of Marriage and the Family* 46 (Aug. 1984): 566; Merlin B. Brinkerhoff and Marlene Mackie, "Religion and Gender: A Comparison of Canadian and American

Second, for periods of time, specific religious denominations have managed to sustain "heroic" exercises in family affirmation: Catholics from 1945 to 1967; Mormons in the 1970s. Yet these experiences have been time limited and have eventually collapsed again toward the middle. Third, the active forces subverting profamily religious behavior appear to be both doctrinal compromise with modernity and economic pressures to complete the industrialization of the home economy and draw all women into the paid labor force.

Student Attitudes", *Journal of Marriage and the Family* 47 (May 1985): 422–23; Mosher and Hendershot, "Religious Factors", 673; and Yoder, "Religion as a Determinant of Fertility", 284–85.

Five

The "Cold War" Family

Another possible solution to the work-home quandary involved the socializing of family functions along the lines of patriotic nationalism. If religion was not quite up to the long-term task of sustaining the family in the modern age, then perhaps American nationalism could successfully fill the void.

This approach acquired a certain urgency in the middle decades of this century, as the United States assumed the role of international "super power". Harvard University's Talcott Parsons, perhaps the most influential sociologist of his generation, emphasized that the stakes were high. The Cold War with the Soviets, he said, was at once a national security problem needing political solution and a domestic problem challenging the legitimacy of "the American way". Indeed, a "major problem" facing the United States was "motivating large sectors of the population *to the level of national effort required to sustain a position of world leadership* in a very unstable and rapidly changing situation". Mobilization to meet the dangers of communism brought "an enormous increase in pressure to subordinate private interests to the public interest". The situation demanded "a stringent display of loyalty going to lengths far beyond our tradition of individual liberty". He viewed the "remarkably uniform, basic type of family" in America, the nuclear family, as the necessary pivot for this expression of loyalty.[1]

[1] Talcott Parsons, *The Social System* (New York: Free Press, 1951), 188; Parsons, "An Outline of the Social System", in *Theories of Society: Foundations of Modern Sociological Theory*, vol. 1, ed. Parsons et al. (New York: Free Press, 1961), 39; and Parsons, "The Normal American Family", in *Man and Civilization: The Family's Search for Survival*, ed. Seymour M. Parker (New York: McGraw-Hill, 1965), 31f.

111

Economic historian (and later national security adviser) Walt W. Rostow was far more enthusiastic and specific about the imperative need for a conformist family order. Writing in 1957, he celebrated America's "set of social conventions which exact a high degree of conformity". Long-term social trends, he argued, would solidify these developments. The average American, Rostow noted, was increasingly a resident of the suburbs. The "white collar experience of the office" was more typical than that of factory or farm. With the end of mass immigration, the spread of industrialization to the South, and geographic mobility, there had been "a marked increase in the social homogeneity of the American population". At the same time, the pressures of the Cold War had imparted "a strand of garrison life to the society as a whole", yet had also "converged with many of the trends built into our domestic dynamics", including suburbanization, bureaucratization, social homogenization, and the political application of the social sciences. The "baby boom", he continued, could be attributed to both the "welfare state" and "garrison state" mentalities active in America. In this new America, Rostow emphasized that "[t]he public and private sectors of our lives cannot be clearly separated." Instead, the new American norm of a managerial, family-centered middle class gave a kind of unity and purpose to American actions overseas. [2]

This vision of a patriotic, garrison-styled American middle class took firmest root in the American armed forces of the Cold War era, 1948 to 1970. Philosophers of the military system noted that the services had made a fundamental shift from an elite, "bachelor", masculine force dedicated to the directed use of force into a "married", "familistic", managerial institution rooted in a web of social and sexual relations and bound together by a common dependency on the state. The creation of

[2] Walt W. Rostow, "The National Style", in *The American Style: Essays in Value and Performance,* ed. Elting E. Morrison (New York: HarperCollins, 1958), 246–313.

this new model of family and state interaction was, in its way, also heroic—another attempt to defy the experience of the past and the pressures of modern economics.

The relationship of the military to family life stood, in fact, as a very old social issue. The perennial problem was how to reconcile the military demand for the total obedience, instantaneous availability, frequent movement, and extended service of the soldier with the individual's innate desire to marry, create a household, and have children. Over time, the preferred military solution had always been to avoid the matter by relying on a bachelor force, except for senior officers. For example, the Roman emperors and the Roman senate before them fought long to preserve a bachelor legion, fearing the consequences of numerous dependents hampering the ranks.[3] Historically, for republics, or republics in the process of becoming empires, the crisis point seemed to come when the army was transformed from a small, elite force supplemented by the mass mobilization of a citizen reserve during emergencies into a large, peacetime standing army.

In the early years of the American republic, the military's relationship to family life derived from the professional code of the eighteenth-century European officers corps: officers took care of their own. Although it was assumed that enlisted men would never marry, it was also informally recognized that senior noncommissioned officers often did. From 1775 to as late as 1947, these assumptions held surprisingly firm. Beginning with the American Revolution and Indian Wars, and through the mass mobilizations of the Civil War, World War I, and World War II, the American armed services remained elite, largely bachelor forces, supplemented in emergencies by state militias and rapid buildups. Until 1942, for example, U.S. Army regulations forbade the peacetime enlistment or reenlistment of men with wives or children. "Military wife" meant

[3] See Brian Campbell, "The Marriage of Soldiers under the Empire", *Journal of Roman Studies* 68 (1978): 155–56.

"officer's wife". Even among the commissioned ranks, men normally delayed marriage until ages 30 to 35 and then commonly married "within the services" to the daughters of senior officers. The services did not recognize the existence of military dependents until the Spanish-American War of 1898, when Congress first granted allotments to the families of enlisted men. Allotments for officers' families came only in 1917.

Women were systematically excluded from the regular military ranks throughout this period. A small Nurses Corps created in 1901, the use of uniformed stenographers in World War I, and the creation of noncombat WAC and WAVE auxiliaries in World War II were the exceptions. For their part, officers' wives served as informal social relations managers on isolated military posts, working to bring a smattering of "culture" to otherwise rough, masculine domains. For a short period even after World War II, some planners anticipated a fairly complete demobilization of the war-swollen services and a return to this prewar pattern.

It was the emergence of the Cold War in 1947–48 that brought the fundamental break in American tradition. In the new atmosphere of crisis and growing international commitment, the centuries-old American aversion to a large standing army was put aside. Defenders of the Republic had always feared a large peacetime national army, which they saw as a threat to political liberties and regional loyalties. In the wrong hands, they also believed, a mass army's temptation to become an integrator of values could threaten the foundations of freedom.

Although few gave the matter much attention at the time, this creation of a large peacetime force also posed the standard problems relative to family life. Whereas the 1890 army of 24,700 officers and men could realistically remain a bachelor force, the same could not be true of a force numbering over a million. For about two charmed decades, though, this development coincided with an upsurge in family life throughout America, with uniquely important military results.

Opinion makers in the immediate postwar years saw the construction of a "new American family" as critical to national identity. At the intellectual level, prominent sociologists called for "a recreated system of family values" and education directed at "building strong, wholesome family life", with women focused on creating "a successful home, one which will exemplify all of the principles of democratic living desired by the community and the nation". They encouraged the emergence of a "uniform family" in America, the nuclear family rooted in a complex, gender-based division of labor.[4] Psychologist John Bowlby's influential book *Maternal Care and Mental Health* had particular influence in the United States. He stressed the need of children for the "warm, intimate, and continuous care of the mother" — "the provision of constant attention day and night, seven days a week, and 365 in the year" — as the foundation of moral character and mental health.[5] At the popular level, too, the image shapers reinforced the vision of the reconstructed American family. Henry Luce used the pages of *Life* in the late 1940s to trumpet the dawn of a "New America", celebrating in particular the surging American birthrate, the new suburbs, an impressive conformity, and the growing number of middle-class families.[6]

These themes merged with and reinforced another reality of postwar American life: the presence of vast numbers of military veterans socialized in the military ethos. The retention of a large peacetime standing army meant that the normal Ameri-

[4] Carle C. Zimmerman, *The Family of Tomorrow: The Cultural Crisis and the Way Out* (New York: Harper & Brothers, 1949), 231; Grace Reaves, "The New Family in the Postwar World", *Marriage and Family Living* 7 (Winter 1945): 73–76; and Parsons, "Normal American Family", 31–49.

[5] John Bowlby, *Maternal Care and Mental Health* (New York: Schocken Books, 1950), 11, 67, 73–74.

[6] See Allan Carlson, "Luce, *Life,* and 'The American Way'", in *The Best of "This World"*, ed. Michael A. Scully (Lanham, MD: University Press of America, 1986), 384–402.

can male experience of the 1940–70 period would include military service in late adolescence or early adulthood. By 1970, roughly half of the 50 million employed U.S. males were veterans, men shaped by a common training in a closed male system.[7] Indeed, the underlying values of military service — conformity, competition, and aggression — became in many respects the civilian ethos of the Cold War era, with the military man easily transformed into a "corporate man", an "organization man" ready to join the managerial institutions of modern life. Under the pressures of Cold War and permanent mobilization, the civilian world was partially militarized, whereas the military world was partially "familized".

As soldiers and sailors, these men had shared a common initiation into manhood. Cut off during basic training from parents and sweethearts, they had entered a world that placed a premium on high physical standards and looked askance at emotion. A restricted masculine environment was deemed necessary to foster the bonds of fellowship and loyalty that would hold small units together in periods of stress and build a servicewide esprit. The military also attempted, usually with success, to complete the socialization of the man as "warrior" before letting his family come back into his life.

During the training phase, the ideal woman remained at home, supporting her young man by letters and gift packages "in tribute to the deprivation [he] is undergoing for her own well-being and that of the nation".[8] But once the new soldier had become part of the system, women assumed a well-defined new role. They rarely came as peers, for a 1948 law limited the number of women in the WAC and WAVE auxiliaries to no more than 2 percent of total enlisted strength. The actual numbers were usually less, and the special corps themselves became notorious for the presence of "secret societies" of lesbians

[7] Noted in Lynne R. Dobrofsky and William Arkin, "Military Socialization and Masculinity", unpublished paper (Dec. 1976), 20. On file at Military Family Resource Center, Arlington, VA.

[8] Ibid., 17.

(who did, in their own way, however, also revel in the masculine qualities of the services and posed no threat to that underlying spirit). [9]

Rather, in the new Cold War era, the military services sought to socialize wives and children into a modified version of the military model, regularizing their role as a kind of special support system. In contrast to the civilian world, military life was ideally suited for the building of a social order that could result in less tension between workplace and home. In this milieu, women should be cast as associate members of the services, with their status fixed by their husband's rank and their roles prescribed by an elaborate code of conduct.

For officer's wives, this basically meant adapting existing unwritten customs for mass guidance and education. These tasks were accomplished by the military etiquette books that poured out after 1945. Inhaling deeply the spirit of the Cold War, Helen Todd Westpheling's *Army Lady Today* stressed that just as wives "esteem, respect, and dignify the estate and sanctity of marriage", so they extended these sentiments "to the integrity and justice of the boundless frontier of democracy our country represents". [10] The most important of these books, perhaps, was Nancy Shea's *The Army Wife,* the "unofficial Bible" commonly presented by the new West Point graduate to his bride. [11] Shea emphasized how a wife's full-time support of her husband represented "an important part in our national security, and a duty to your country". Wives must build "a congenial, happy home life" to soothe the soldier on his return. "Homemaking is a full-time job, and a wife should not work if such work

[9] Brian Mitchell, *Weak Link: The Feminization of the American Military* (Washington, DC: Regnery Gateway, 1989), 178–82.

[10] Helen Todd Westpheling, *Army Lady Today* (Charlotte, NC: Heritage House, 1959), 7.

[11] See Elizabeth M. Finlayson, "A Study of the Wife of the Military Officer: Her Academic and Career Preparation, Her Current Employment and Volunteer Services", in *Families in the Military System,* ed. Hamilton I. McCubbin, Barbara B. Dahl, and Edna J. Hunter (Newbury Park, CA: Sage, 1976), 23.

in any way jeopardizes her home responsibilities." Given the demands of military life, the army wife must be prepared to bear "the responsibility of being both mother and father" to her children.[12] Addressing Navy wives, Anne Briscoe Pye joined Shea in endorsing the production of "Navy Juniors", or children, as "the most important job of your life, the one for which you were designed".[13] All of these books gave instruction on the elaborate social customs expected of an officer's wife, from formal calls on the post commander's spouse, to afternoon teas, to volunteer work through the Officers' Wives Clubs found on every post.[14]

The necessary socialization of families of enlisted men occurred in a more direct, statist manner. The services crafted a comprehensive welfare system, involving the steady expansion of benefits, which turned both the man and his family into "military dependents". Military planners reasoned that adequate welfare benefits would usefully insulate personnel from the outside world, provide a sense of security, foster morale, and encourage an attitude of solidarity: all the attributes of a successful socialist order. In 1942, Public Law 77-490 extended for the first time special medical benefits to military dependents, including some obstetrical care. The same year witnessed creation of Army Emergency Relief (AER), designed to relieve distress among Army members and their families. Post Exchange stores, enjoying a number of hidden subsidies, offered goods at discounted costs. The 1952 Wickenden Study highlighted the lack of basic military social services, leading, in part, to the extension of full health benefits to all military dependents through the Dependents Medical Care Act of 1956. On-base housing construction mushroomed in the 1950s. Meanwhile,

[12] Nancy Shea, *The Army Wife,* 4th ed. (New York: Harper & Row, 1966), 1, 4–5, 135.

[13] Anne Briscoe Pye and Nancy B. Shea, *The Navy Wife,* revised by Barbara Naylor (New York and London: Harper & Row, 1965), 114.

[14] See Mary Preston Gross, *Mrs. Lieutenant* (Sausalito, CA: Graphic Arts of Marin, 1968).

the army opened a series of day-care centers on both domestic and foreign posts, designed "to enhance the morale of servicemen and their families". The services reached a milestone in 1960, as family members outnumbered uniformed personnel in the active force for the first time. This led to the creation of umbrella organizations for family services: the Army Community Service (ACS) Program and its naval and air equivalents. In 1966, the Civilian Health and Medical Program of the Uniformed Services (CHAMPUS) again expanded the availability of government-backed medical care. This uniquely military form of socialism encompassed an evergrowing number of Americans.[15]

There is little doubt that this collection of reworked customs bonded to health and welfare benefits had profamily intent and effect. For officers, marriage came to be considered vital for career advancement, and divorce was considered detrimental.[16] The ability of wives to take part in military social rituals and volunteer work had a powerful effect on their husbands' advancement and success.[17] And military benefits had a clear pronatalist structure. Military housing, for example, was allotted by a combination of rank and family size and composition, with the largest families drawing the more spacious dwellings. The military medical system paid the direct costs of pregnancy and childbirth at a time when these were out-of-pocket expenses for most civilians. Travel allowances were among the other benefits linked to family size, leading some to complain

[15] A short history of the army welfare system is found in "Chief of Staff, U.S. Army", in *White Paper 1983: The Army Family,* reproduced as Appendix E in *The Army Family Action Plan II,* pamphlet 608-41 (Washington, DC: U.S. Department of the Army, 1985), 31–34.

[16] See Nancy L. Goldman, "Trends in Family Patterns of U.S. Military Personnel During the 20th Century", in *The Social Psychology of Military Service,* ed. Nancy L. Goldman and David R. Segal (Newbury Park, CA: Sage, 1976), 130.

[17] This point is stressed in Esther Wier and Dorothy Coffin Hickey, *The Answer Book on Naval Social Customs* (Harrisburg, PA: Military Services, 1956), 57.

that Pentagon policies were "actively pro-natalist as well as discriminating against those who do not have children".[18]

Did this profamily orientation of the 1948–70 period "work"
in the sense of encouraging traditional family life? In some
respects, the answer is yes. Concerning marriage, military
officers showed a significantly higher propensity to marry than
did civilians. In 1960, 84.9 percent of all officers were married, compared to 69.1 percent of the general adult male population.[19] In his careful study of divorce among U.S. Air Force
officers, sociologist John Williams, Jr., discovered that their rate
of divorce was less than half that of all U.S. males ages 20
through 54 and that this rate held steady throughout the 1963–
69 period, whereas the general divorce rate climbed (in 1963,
the air force rate was 0.45 of the civilian rate; in 1969, 0.37).
He concluded that the officer's "loyalty to the country, to the
Air Force, and to the unit may carry over into loyalty to the
wife" and that the wife in turn felt that she was part of a "team"
and necessary in her own way to the fulfillment of the air force
mission.[20] Similarly, officers' wives showed a significantly
greater attachment to traditional gender roles. A study of army
officers in 1969 showed only 20 percent of their wives to be
currently employed, full or part time, whereas a Defense Department–wide survey a year later of both enlisted and officers'
wives found only 30 percent of them employed, compared to
41 percent in the general population.[21] Confirming this orientation, some researchers also reported that feminism had made
virtually no inroads among military wives by the early 1970s,
a fact attributed to the isolation of military posts, the supportive
network of the military community, and the welfare entitle-

[18] See C. Shannon Stokes and Ralph R. Sell, "Pronatalism and Fertility: The
Case of the Military", *Social Biology* 25 (Winter 1978): 259–61.

[19] Goldman, "Trends in Family Patterns of U.S. Military Personnel", 130.

[20] John Wesley Williams, Jr., "Divorce and Dissolution in the Military Family", in *Families in the Military System,* ed. McCubbin et al., 209–36.

[21] Finlayson, "Study of the Wife of the Army Officer", 35–36; and *White
Paper 1983,* 34.

ments enjoyed by military dependents, all of which combined to prevent "alienation". [22]

Concerning family size, some data suggested that military families bore more children than did their civilian counterparts. One report from the early 1970s found that the average military family had more children under 18 years of age (1.62 children) than eleven civilian occupational groups. However, a more sophisticated study, which introduced controls for income, race, age, and education, could find "no evidence to support the effect on fertility of pro-natalist incentives in the military". [23] Research did suggest, though, that each of the services formed a unique community, with career families regularly choosing to use post services and resources instead of civilian counterparts. In general, military families took part in "a distinct, informal, subcultural care-taking system" built on a security-oriented benefit program and composed of close-knit families that shared basic values. [24]

But therein lay the weakness of this alternative: the potential spread or imposition of an alternate set of values that would disrupt the delicate balance achieved between military work and the family and also threaten the traditions and psychology needed by an effective military force. Multiple challenges came in the 1967–73 period, each independent in its own way, yet mutually reinforcing and revolutionary in their scope. They destroyed the military-family balance achieved in the 1950s and left the military services in social and cultural disarray.

One challenge derived from the national disillusionment over

[22] Lynne R. Dobrofsky, "The Wife: From Military Dependent to Feminist?" in *Changing Families in a Changing Military System,* ed. Edna Hunter, DTIC No. AO67-628 (San Diego, CA: Naval Health Research Center, 1977), 39.

[23] Goldman, "Trends in Family Patterns of U.S. Military Personnel", 128–29; and Stokes and Sell, "Pronatalism and Fertility", 268–69.

[24] Frank Flores Montalvo, "Family Separation in the Army: A Study of the Problems Encountered and the Correlating Resources Used by Career Army Families Undergoing Military Separation", in *Families in the Military System,* ed. McCubbin et al., 168–70.

Vietnam. Between 1948 and 1972, the services had maintained their ranks, in part, through use of the draft. However, the Indochinese stalemate drained support for the system, and Richard Nixon's 1968 electoral victory was based, in part, on the Republican Party's pledge to end conscription. Nixon's subsequent Commission on an All-Volunteer Armed Force, headed by Thomas S. Gates, Jr., confidently concluded that higher pay and other improvements in service life could make an all-volunteer force (AVF) possible.

The manpower demands of the war, linked to the politicians' reluctance to call up the reserves, led to another fundamental shift in military policy. In 1966, the Pentagon established a task force to reassess the role of women in the armed forces, to include "the potential for greater employment, recruitment, and retention, especially in relation to current skill requirements of the buildup for Southeast Asia and other deployments". Legislation the following year removed the cap of 2 percent on the number of women in the enlisted ranks. A few years later, military planners and politicians grew unnerved by the supposed "manpower crunch" said to loom in the latter 1970s, as the "baby boomers" gave way to the "baby bust" generation. In short, badly shaken politicians turned toward women as the means of ending the unpopular draft while still maintaining Cold War military force levels.[25]

The consequences of this planned expansion in the use of women were few, however, until further stimulated by the revived American feminist movement. The long ineffective Defense Advisory Committee on Women in the Services (or DACOWITS), for example, imbibed this new brew and became a kind of feminist lobby pushing for an expanded female presence in the services, including combat.[26]

[25] See William Bowman, Roger Little, and G. Thomas Sicilia, *The All-Volunteer Force After a Decade: Retrospect and Prospect* (Washington, DC: Pergamon-Brassey's International Defense Publishers, 1986), 82.

[26] Mitchell, *Weak Link,* 22–24.

More generally, though, American feminists found themselves torn over the question of military service. As political scientist Jean Bethke Elshtain explained: "From its inception, feminism has not quite known whether to lament sex differences and deny their importance or to acknowledge and even valorize such differences; whether to condemn all wars outright or to extol women's contributions to war efforts."[27]

Although some American feminists adhered to an absolute pacifism,[28] the bulk of the movement eventually resolved to push for the full integration of women into the services, including combat arms. The military family system, distrusted by the movement for its traditional and pronatalist aspects, became an indirect target. Feminist theorists believed that they could undermine the military shield that screened military families from civilian influence. With a small but significant minority of military wives already identifying with feminism, with more women soon to join the ranks, and with the possibility of more married military couples, the existing order seemed fragile. As one writer explained: "It appears that the very mechanisms of social control which the military has successfully employed regarding the military wife (guilt, responsibility for husband's career, etc.) are those which feminism promises to threaten the most."[29]

This revolution broke into the open in 1972, shortly after Congress approved the Equal Rights Amendment (E.R.A.) by overwhelming margins and with all the pundits predicting that the states would ratify it quickly. Fearful that existing policies regarding the enlistment and assignment of women would soon be unconstitutional, Pentagon planners hoped to make a more

[27] Jean Bethke Elshtain, *Women and War* (New York: Basic Books, 1987), 231.

[28] See Wendy Chapkis, *Loaded Questions: Women in the Military* (Amsterdam/Washington, DC: Transnational Institute, 1981).

[29] Dobrofsky, "The Wife", 42.

gradual adjustment to the new egalitarian realities and further resolved to make a virtue of necessity. [30]

The feminist impulse also found fertile native ground. Some research pointed to a latent sympathy among officers' wives for the E.R.A., one survey reporting that 85 percent of those questioned supported its passage. [31] Edna Hunter, a veteran of military family studies, speculated in 1982 that the Cold War family system had actually spawned the attitudes now shaking its foundations: whereas the military wife had been expected to place herself in service to her husband's and the military's needs, the system also required "an independent, self-sustaining, liberated woman" if it was to accomplish the mission. This tension simply could not hold forever. [32]

With their reputations and careers on the line, Pentagon personnel planners also worked with unusual zeal to make the process a success. Military advertising directed at women turned feminist rhetoric into recruiting slogans (e.g., "Today's Army Is Leading the Way in Opportunities for Women"). Women were integrated into basic combat training, where female troopers, moving shoulder to shoulder with male comrades through rifle, grenade, and bayonet training, fulfilled many activist dreams. The critical symbolic change came in 1975, when Congress approved a measure opening Annapolis, West Point, and Colorado Springs to women. Opposition to this move by the commandants of the academies had been intense, resting on the argument that the service schools aimed at training combat leaders, roles currently not open to women. However, Con-

[30] See Mady Wechsler Segal and David R. Segal, "Social Change and the Participation of Women in the American Military", unpublished paper prepared for the Department of Military Psychiatry (Washington, DC: Walter Reed Army Institute of Research, 1981), 27.

[31] Carolyn J. Becraft, "The Women's Movement: Its Effects on the Wives of Military Officers", unpublished paper (Los Angeles: University of Southern California, 1978), 36. On file at Military Family Resource Center, Arlington, VA.

[32] Edna J. Hunter, *Families Under the Flag: A Review of Military Family Literature* (New York: Praeger, 1982), 10.

gress resolved that "basic education" was in fact the primary purpose of these schools. Accordingly, women must be let in.

The service academies thereby joined the coeducational "academic revolution" marking the late 1960s and embarked on "one of the most radical experiments in equalitarianism ever tried in American education".[33] Planners assumed that the relative ease with which the academies had achieved racial integration several decades earlier could be replicated through a sex integration process based on the premise of androgyny: that there are few real differences and no militarily significant differences between men and women. The all-male atmosphere of the academies and the idea of "male bonding" as critical to military success came to be viewed as anachronisms. Starting in 1976, unusually "traditional" young men were combined with decidedly nontraditional young women in a dramatic challenge to the eliteness, maleness, and traditions of the primal military institutions.[34]

The overall process advanced rapidly. By 1980, with 171,400 women in uniform (8.4 percent of the total), the U.S. armed forces had more women in service than any other country. Similarly, more of these women were in "nontraditional" and near-combat jobs than anywhere else in the world, including the egalitarian socialist Swedish Army and the nearly mythical Israeli Defense Force. Plans fixed by the Carter administration in 1980 looked to a female force level of 265,000 by FY 1986.[35]

Undergirding this triumphant march of ideological androgyny was a more basic change in military philosophy. In an influential paper given at the 1973 meeting of the American Sociological Association, Charles Moskos noted, almost in passing, that the American military was going through an "organiza-

[33] Robert F. Priest, Allan G. Vitters, and Howard T. Prince, "Coeducation at West Point", *Armed Forces and Society* 4 (Aug. 1978): 591–92.

[34] Lois B. DeFleur, David Gillman, and William Marshak, "Sex Integration of the U.S. Air Force Academy: Changing Roles for Women", *Armed Forces and Society* 4 (Aug. 1978): 608, 613, 616; and Mitchell, *Weak Link,* 50, 67, 80–83.

[35] Bowman et al., *All-Volunteer Force After a Decade,* 83–85.

tional shift from a predominantly institutional format (i.e., legitimated by normative values) to one more resembling that of an occupation (i.e., akin to civilian marketplace standards)".[36] Pentagon planners and military theorists seized on this idea of a change from "institutionalism" to "careerism", finding it to be an effective rationale for policies already in place. A year earlier, for example, General Creighton Abrams had relaxed army duty standards, granting more civilian-type freedoms during off-duty hours in order to make military life comparable to civilian life.[37] Others reasoned that the "masculine values" surrounding basic training could be muted or eliminated. In the all-volunteer force, they believed, the military no longer represented a training ground for boys to become men, but rather a vocation center for careers for which men and women volunteered.[38]

Theorists in the Department of Military Psychiatry, Walter Reed Army Institute of Research, argued that technological change had overwhelmed the old "mobilization model" of defense, resting on an elite force supplemented by a mobilized reserve. The advent of air power and nuclear weapons, a blurred distinction between military and civilian, and the miniaturization of weapons brought fundamental change, reducing the difference between "wartime" and "peacetime", mandating a large professionalized standing force, and making "war fighting" in the classic sense unlikely. Rather, service in the modern military was said to be more like police work and amenable to regular hours and careerist paths.[39]

Sociologist Lois B. DeFleur, a key service consultant in the sex integration of the Air Force Academy, stressed that in the

[36] Charles C. Moskos, "Studies on the American Soldier", paper presented at the annual meeting of the American Sociological Association, New York, Aug. 1973, as quoted in Segal and Segal, "Social Change", 8.

[37] M. Stanton Duncan, "The Military Family: Its Future in the All-Volunteer Context", in *The Social Psychology of Military Service,* ed. Goldman and Segal, 138.

[38] Dobrofsky and Arkin, "Military Socialization and Masculinity", 20.

[39] Segal and Segal, "Social Change", 22.

late twentieth century, "[t]here is less need for individuals to lead troops and a growing demand for managers and diplomats."[40] These truths, the analysts agreed, reinforced the turn toward women. For whereas male recruits still exhibited the old-fashioned patriotic orientation, women recruits gave emphasis to self-advancement and career strategies, approaches in consonance with the new order of things.[41]

More fundamental than this shift in guiding military philosophy, though, was the manner in which the American military became a conscious tool used by social engineers to guide domestic society. A common development seen in Third World countries is the military's self-categorization as the "vanguard of modernization", with a superior ability to steamroll traditional ways and "deliver social change". Under intense pressures, the American military began assuming the same function. Writing in 1978, Harvard sociologist M. D. Feld described the newly recognized role of the U.S. armed forces as instruments of social innovation, highlighting their "ambitious" goal "of eliminating the belief that there is a natural and all-pervasive sexually based distinction between the wielders and the objects of coercion". Although the American military had been slow to awake to this role (e.g., "The Great War was a social revolution, but an aborted one"), the Cold War's unique bonding of sustained militarism to the expanded welfare state gave social planners a powerful tool to effect change:

> One consequence of the contemporary fusion of the notions of national security and national welfare has been the sensible eradication of the conceptual distinction between the nation-in-arms and the nation at peace. The notion of total mobilization as the archetypal wartime measure is on the way out. It is being replaced by the model of the permanently mobilized state: a state

[40] DeFleur et al., "Sex Integration of the U.S. Air Force Academy", 617.
[41] Jack M. Hicks, "Women in the U.S. Army", *Armed Forces and Society* 4 (Aug. 1978): 650.

mobilized not for reasons of war, but in order to allocate its
resources in the fullest and most rational manner possible.[42]

Under this merger of the welfare state and the national security state, the soldier "is no longer the mobilized common man,
but a career civil servant". Feld admitted that the introduction
of women into the services would destroy "the elitist notions
that motivate combat performance", but these bore, in any case,
little relationship to modern realities. Rather, historical evolution had produced a permanently mobilized society pursuing
the "consensus goal" of "social or civil equality".[43]

Similarly, Colonel Shirley Bach of the Defense Equal Opportunity Management Institute celebrated sex integration of
the military as a splendid opportunity for applied social engineering: "It is a process that could be as effectively managed as the development and introduction of a new weapons
system if the proper variables and information are considered
and if appropriate priorities are set." She acknowledged the
disruptive impact of the integration process at the academies
and the negative effect on military preparedness. Nonetheless,
she said, the process must go forward.[44] Indeed, on discover-
ing that male cadets in the first sex-integrated class of the Air
Force Academy grew, over time, more hostile to women in
the military and more traditional in sex role attitudes, the air
force simply accelerated efforts at social engineering. This
involved the introduction of more "high-status" women as
trainers and the institution of integrated housing.[45] In short,
the use of the military as a vehicle for mandatory social change

[42] M. D. Feld, "Arms and the Woman: Some General Considerations", *Armed
Forces and Society* 4 (Aug. 1978): 563.

[43] Ibid., 565–67.

[44] Shirley J. Bach, "Women in the Military: Planning and Managing the
Process of Change", paper presented at the Twentieth Anniversary National
Inter-University Seminar, University of Chicago, Oct. 25, 1980.

[45] Lois B. DeFleur and David Gillman, "Cadet Beliefs, Attitudes, and In-
teractions during the Early Phases of Sex Integration", *Youth and Society* 10
(Dec. 1978): 188.

and the primary valuation given to the visions of androgyny and "equal opportunity" became by 1980 the equivalent of military gospel.

What changes in the military-family balance did these social and ideological challenges bring? At one level, change appeared to be minimal. For example, American soldiers, sailors, and airmen continued to marry earlier and produce more children earlier than their civilian counterparts, differences sustained through the late 1980s.[46] At a deeper level, though, the changes were numerous and involved:

1. *The decline of traditional family life.* By 1980, the air force could report that the traditional family was disappearing from its ranks. Only 19 percent of personnel were in "traditional families", composed of an air force father, nonworking civilian wife and mother, and one or more children. Even when excluding the unmarried, traditional families so defined counted for only 28 percent of all air force families.[47] Senior naval officers reported that young ensigns and lieutenants no longer enjoyed the support of their wives. Said one naval aviation commander, "I don't understand the young wives. They are ruining these guys' careers."[48] Officers' Wives Clubs, organizational symbols of traditional women's roles in the Cold War army, withered everywhere in the 1970s. Even those that survived seemed to have turned primarily to the support of rape crisis, battered wives, or child-care centers. Along with their political lobbying for expanded military benefits, club members

[46] See Community and Family Support Center, U.S. Department of the Army, *Army Family Action Plan: Research and Evaluation, Annual Report, 1987,* memorandum (Feb. 12, 1988), 5, 8.

[47] Office of the Chief of Staff, U.S. Department of the Air Force, *Air Force Conference on Families, 24–26 September 1980. Conference Report and Family Action Plan* (Washington, DC: U.S. Department of the Air Force, 1980?), 3.

[48] C. Brooklyn Derr, "Marriage/Family Issues and Wife Styles across Naval Career Stages: Their Implications for Career Success", technical paper no. 2, sponsored by the Organizational Effectiveness Research Program (Washington, DC: U.S. Office of Naval Research, 1981), 13.

had effectively joined the new order.[49] At the same time, commentators speculated that the most important strains within the army's organization might well be "those developing in the homes of military personnel between husbands and wives".[50]

2. *The rise of "pluralistic families"*. As the obverse side of traditional family decline, "new family forms", such as dual-career couples and single-parent families, predominated in the services. Among the growing female ranks, pregnancy in and out of wedlock became common. In 1980, 16 percent of all women in the U.S. Army were pregnant. Substantial numbers of young single women also joined the services, aware that their dependents would receive health benefits, basic subsistence allowances, subsidized child care, and commissary and BX/PX privileges.[51] At the same time, growing levels of daily male-female interaction led to a burgeoning growth in "service couples", with both husband and wife in the ranks. By 1988, 50,000 couples, or 100,000 service members, were in this new category. More broadly, the percentage of military spouses (still mostly wives) in the general labor market climbed from 30 percent in 1970 (compared to 41 percent of civilians) to 52 percent in 1980 (compared to 51 percent of civilians). According to a study by the Rand Corporation, this was "the most significant change in Army family structure" during the period.[52]

[49] Jay Finegan, "Wives Clubs: Can They Survive the '80s?" *The [Army] Times Magazine* (Aug. 3, 1981): 6–10; and Jane Sobie, "Wives Clubs in the 1980's: A New Perspective", *Ladycom* (Sept. 1981): 97–98.

[50] Ellywyn R. Stoddard and Claude E. Cabanillas, "The Army Officer's Wife: Social Stresses in a Complementary Role", in *Social Psychology of Military Science,* ed. Goldman and Segal, 153.

[51] Cecile S. Landrum, "The Conflicts Surrounding Family and Children versus Mission Responsibilities: What Are the Impacts on Readiness?" paper presented at the Joint Interversity Seminar—Air University Symposium on "Changing Military Manpower Realities" (Montgomery, AL: Maxwell Air Force Base, June 3–5, 1979), 8.

[52] U.S. Department of the Army, *The Army Family Action Plan V* (Washington, DC: U.S. Department of the Army, 1988), 14.

3. *Greater "socialization" of the military family.* In a career- and training-oriented military system, benefits became the driving force in recruitment and retention. Despite the construction of a crude socialist order during the Cold War era, the all-volunteer force and its pluralistic families demanded ever more, specifically child-care and youth services. Although military spokesmen sometimes lamented that the services were not "surrogate parents", the surging number of service couples, joint-career couples, and single mothers with dependent children made child management a critical military issue. Edna Hunter concluded that "the provision of child care for military families may be essential today for mission readiness", and she gave her blessing to a new air force experiment providing twenty-four-hour child-care availability to base commanders in case of alerts. [53] The Army Family Action Plan of 1987 described "the availability of quality child developmental care" as being "a crucial program for the Army". [54] Indeed, the demand for subsidized infant and child care became an incessant military chant, coming both from unit commanders concerned about readiness and regular personnel, who claimed that they could no longer meet obligations to their children. [55] By 1988, the army operated 581 child-care centers on 412 installations, with a direct subsidy of $80 million. As one recent army report declared: "The Child Care Program is undergoing dynamic change as we work to upgrade existing facilities, plan for the construction of new physical plants, develop separate career fields for childcare professionals, and refine job standards and training." [56] At the same time, the Department of the Army complained that "the

[53] Hunter, *Families Under the Flag,* 55.

[54] *Army Family Action Plan, 1987* (1988), 8.

[55] See *Navy Family Awareness Conference. Interim Report* (Jan. 1979), 2, III-2; and the Association of the United States Army, *The Army Family: Analysis and Appraisal: Proceedings of a Symposium* (Washington, DC: U.S. Department of the Army, 1980), 16–17.

[56] *Army Family Action Plan II* (1985), 37.

problems of spouse employment are growing faster than the solutions." One response was simply to encourage the trend by opening Army Community Services spouse employment programs on military posts. In 1985, 56,538 spouses received this aid; in 1986, 135,674.[57]

4. *The erosion of military community.* Although military families' dependence on government programs increased, the sense of broader community that once animated the military brotherhood appeared to dissolve. The closed, tight, interdependent world of the Cold War family gave way to a careerist orientation in which military service was increasingly a job, not an adventure or even a priority commitment. Researchers reported that military men wanted more time to be with their children and were less willing to tolerate twenty-four-hour-a-day service. Military spouses, for their part, were far less willing to serve as an informal support network, and the average number of volunteer hours given by service families steadily declined. At the same time, military personnel wanted their own homes, and by the mid-1980s, 70 percent of families lived off post. The cumulative effect was the steady decay in a sense of community. As one air force report lamented: "Even though many services are provided and an Air Force community is readily available, more than half of the family members interviewed report that they have no close friends, neighbors, or work associates."[58] Rather, family members became more isolated as they pursued careers and became increasingly dependent on a diffuse web of military benefits.

5. *The desperate quest for a military family policy.* By 1980, a clear sense of family crisis haunted the services. On the one

[57] See *Army Family Action Plan, 1987* (1988), 15.

[58] *Air Force Conference on Families* (Sept. 24–26, 1980), 49. Also Hunter, *Families Under the Flag,* 6, 9; *Army Family Action Plan, 1987* (1988), 16; and Gary J. Norbo, Richard S. Seeberg, and William L. Wubbens, Jr., "Trends in the Structure of Army Families", *Journal of Political and Military Sociology* 4 (Spring 1976): 138.

hand, military planners saw mounting evidence that the combat readiness of many units was seriously impaired by the absence of personnel due to the conflicts of family responsibilities. Despite regulations requiring service couples with dependents and single parents to make advance provision for the care of their children during alerts, relatively few did so.[59] During these events, many actually brought their children along. As one researcher laconically observed: "This is probably the worst time to have children underfoot — especially where National Security is concerned."[60] Interviews with service personnel showed that many believed there would never be a war, while others declared that in a real emergency, they were staying home with the children.[61]

On the other hand, there was a kind of ferment at the military "grass-roots", reflected in signs among the ranks indicating a system badly out of kilter. In 1980, a group of officers' wives convened the first Army-Wide Family Symposium. Similar sessions were held in 1981 and 1982, sponsored by the newly organized Family Action Committee. The navy and air force witnessed similar gatherings in the same period. Thousands of voices at these assemblies complained about new stress and complexities in their lives, yet they could find solutions only in expanded benefits: more employment assistance for military spouses, better health and dental care, expanded free transportation, enhanced youth activities, and improved military child care.

With a sense of urgency and unease, the services embraced the social sciences and spawned a curious series of documents that combined traditional Pentagonese with the jargon and agenda of politicized sociology. Army initiatives set the pattern. In his 1983 "White Paper", *The Army Family,* Chief of Staff John A. Wickham, Jr., laid out the new army family philosophy:

[59] *Air Force Conference on Families* (Sept. 24–26, 1980), 57.
[60] Landrum, "Conflicts Surrounding Family and Children", 17.
[61] Ibid.

"Towards the goal of building a strong partnership [between the army and army families], the Army remains committed to assuring adequate support to families to promote wellness; develop a sense of community; and strengthen the mutually reinforcing bonds between the Army and its families." With the intent of fostering "Army families of excellence", the White Paper focused on "wellness", which implied in turn "prevention and building of family strengths". This required the identification of "stressors for families" and led military planners to advance an array of new programs in the areas of health care, child development, incest and suicide prevention, youth counseling, and so on.

The first comprehensive Family Action Plan, issued in 1984, "The Year of the Army Family", implemented dozens of specific initiatives that greatly expanded the military's presence in family lives. [62] As one analyst concluded, such a program brought the families of servicemen "even more within the military system", but he saw no real management alternative to this new phase of socialization. [63] Enhanced benefits, increased family dependence on the state, and more therapeutic counseling would help merge individual families into the "Total Army Family". [64]

6. *The feminization of the armed services.* Although mounting numbers of women soldiers were part of this equation, a more critical change came through the shift in the military's psychological emphasis, from controlled use of force to caring. Even among the traditional service families, researchers could identify "the increasing influence of wives" on military practices and a strengthening of the matriarchal family structure already brought on by the regular disruptions and separations of military service. [65] The army's Family Action Plan for 1988 stressed

[62] See *Army Family Action Plan II* (1985), 4–5, 23, 29, 36–37.
[63] Duncan, "Military Family", 145.
[64] *Army Family Action Plan* (1985), 7.
[65] Duncan, "Military Family", 141; *Army Family Action Plan, 1987* (1988), 4–5.

the need for the sensitivity training of unit leaders in soldier-family relations, child-care problems, and the needs of army infants.[66] Theorists proposed that unit leaders view whole families, not individual soldiers, as the primary unit for management decisions. Meanwhile, unit leadership must shift from a hierarchical, obedience mode to a familial, cooperative one. As one official army statement put it: "We want soldiers, of all ranks, feeling they belong to a 'family'. . . . Building the 'family' requires professional sensitivity toward and caring for one another. . . . We want these professional, caring relationships, because they are necessary to build the vertical bonds which tie leader to led."[67]

7. *A turn to moral engineering.* In its efforts to contain the problems unleashed by the disruption of the Cold War military-family bond, the armed services moved into a new kind of social engineering. Some examples bordered on the humorous, such as published army advice to women soldiers in the field: "Sex does not just happen in the garrison setting. If you are on birth control pills, make sure that you bring enough packs along to last you for the exercises." Others reflected deeper breaks with the whole of human history, including the army's new camouflage maternity uniform. In the desperate drive to retain women in the services, moreover, military leaders even contemplated intentional breaks with traditional morality. As the vice commandant of the Coast Guard explained in testimony on retention problems: "If family rearing is a major factor, we must explore alternatives." Similarly, a Marine Corps study suggested that the corps "help women develop short-term alternatives to marriage and pregnancy for overcoming loneliness", but stopped short of specifying examples.[68]

[66] *Army Family Action Plan V* (1988), 9–10.

[67] Letter from the Adjutant General of the U.S. Army, Nov. 21, 1986, found in Mitchell, *Weak Link,* 221.

[68] See "Feminine Hygiene in the Field Setting", U.S. Army pamphlet; minutes of the DACOWITS spring meeting, 1984, C-7; and Marjorie H. Royle, *Fac-*

Another powerful social engineering tool for the new military was the concept of androgyny. Although acknowledging that normative views of masculinity and femininity had been shaped by American culture and that these views were deep seated and difficult to change, one air force report concluded that they must be eliminated, because they "can interfere with efficient Air Force productivity". Required air force courses on human relations were the tools through which American cultural stereotypes could be uprooted and proper thinking on gender roles put in place.[69]

A major consequence of all these changes was the destabilization of more American families. This process ultimately played out at the individual level, as found in this first-person 1979 account of a female marine sergeant leaving her two children, ages 2 years and 10 months, to accept an overseas posting critical to her career:

> Probably the hardest thing that I ever had to do in my life was to board the plane that July afternoon. After the usual exchange of kisses, I hugged my children for the last time along with my husband and boarded the flight. . . . After having served a couple of weeks here in Okinawa, I'm gradually beginning to accept my situation like countless other Marines on unaccompanied orders have.[70]

As the Gulf War broke out in 1990/91, this became a tale commonly repeated. These soldiers joined the ranks of deracinated American women, separated from their husbands and kin, with

tors *Affecting Attrition among Marine Corps Women* (San Diego, CA: Naval Personnel Research and Development Center, 1985), vii; quotations from Mitchell, *Weak Link,* 171, 175.

[69] Joseph R. Sanchez, "More Women in the Air Force: Implications for Air Force Supervisors", research report no. 465 (Maxwell Air Force Base, AL: Air War College, 1978), 25, 38–45.

[70] Brenda A. Landos, "A Woman Marine Says Goodbye", *Navy Times* (Dec. 31, 1979): 13.

children who would predictably enjoy the regular care of the kinder, gentler Leviathan state.

It is true that the 1980s witnessed a social countermovement, seeking restoration of the Cold War family model. At one level, it appeared that in their egalitarianism, the nation's military planners continued to stumble over certain realities of human nature. Survey data, for example, suggested that enlisted women had become the Achilles' heel of the new American military. Unlike female officers, who exhibited high levels of ideological commitment, most enlisted women continued to desire traditionally female military jobs (e.g., clerk-typist) and aimed at finding a good man, marrying, and having children, often leaving the service at the same time (female enlisted marines had an attrition rate twice that of males). In this sense, they were probably no different than their blue-collar or farm-bound mothers and grandmothers, who turned in their eras to the textile mills or cotton fields for temporary survival. Even some female officers, it turned out, eventually opted out of the military in favor of the nurturing of children.[71] Studies of sex integration at the service academies suggested, moreover, that male cadets grew ever more traditional in their views of women, despite the constant egalitarian pressure.[72]

Yet these pressures failed to ignite an effective countermovement. The Reagan administration did take tentative steps in this direction, implementing in 1981 a "pause" in the planned increase in the number of service women. Beyond that action, though, "the Reagan revolution" in this sphere sputtered and died. The powerful DACOWITS committee, for example, remained a feminist preserve, merely a Republican one now. A planned retrenchment in the number of near-combat army jobs

[71] Joel M. Savell, John C. Woelfel, Barry E. Collins, and Peter M. Bentler, "A Study of Male and Female Soldiers' Beliefs about the 'Appropriateness' of Various Jobs for Women in the Army", *Sex Roles* 5 (1979): 45–46; Landrum, "Conflicts Surrounding Family and Children", 7; and Mitchell, *Weak Link,* 146, 197–99.

[72] DeFleur et al., "Sex Integration of the U.S. Air Force Academy", 617–18.

open to women largely collapsed. Even during the term of Navy Secretary James Webb, a public opponent of the sex integration of the military, the Marine Corps took steps to bring women into Hawk antiaircraft missile battalions and other near-combat jobs, to sex integrate enlisted barracks, and to spend new resources for marine child-care facilities.

As in many areas of public policy, the 1980–89 period marked a slowdown, but nonetheless a failure, in reversing the pace of social change. By decade's end, it was clear that the Cold War family model would not be restored.

Six

The Professional Temptation

The most direct effort to bridge the severed bond of home and work was the creation of a new profession: home economics. Although less important in scope and consequences than the strategies outlined in earlier chapters, the push for a professionalized household economy reveals most vividly the effort to counter the effects of industrialized society on marriage, domesticity, traditional gender roles, and the status of children. For nearly half a century, home economics flourished as a defender of the modern home. Yet in the peculiar cultural environment of the late twentieth century, leading home economists turned rhetorically against home and family, acknowledging in effect the failure of their enterprise. Indeed, closer reflection shows that this odd turn of the profession was not an aberration, but rather the logical result of fundamental weaknesses that took seventy years to resolve.

Home economics grew out of the familiar social fault line of the mid-nineteenth century, in which industrialization had shattered the natural economy of the rural family and separated the workplace from the home. As noted before, it was Catharine Beecher who first tried to wrestle with the implications of the new order. Writing in this period, Beecher argued for a separation of the family from these new economic forces and for the creation within homes of islands of antimodernity in the competitive sea. Only by disaggregating home and work into separate spheres and by linking that division to gender, she reasoned, could decency, love, and the family community survive in the industrial age.

Under these conditions, Beecher wrote, woman was "necessarily the guardian of the nursery, the companion of childhood, and the constant model of imitation". In the new rough-and-

tumble competitive world, the recovery of virtue depended on
the nation's women: "Just as the wives and mothers sink or rise
in the scale of virtue, intelligence and piety, husbands and sons
will rise and fall." Within each home, the woman must become
a self-sacrificing laborer, offering the self-devotion of the strong
and wise on behalf of the weak. Through such gifts, the au-
thor believed, the demoralizing aspects of a competitive market system might be overcome and virtue retained.

The necessary tasks would not be easy. As Beecher noted
in 1835, the nation's public or "common" schools were increasingly viewed as "dangerous places for children", and parents
concerned with their children's moral training were "more and
more withdrawing them from what they deem such contami-
nating influence". Ever mindful of the scope of modernity's
challenge to decency and the natural family economy, Beecher
emphasized the stakes in the struggle: "The great crisis is hasten-
ing on, when it shall be decided whether disenthralled intellect
and liberty shall voluntarily submit to the laws of virtue and
of Heaven, or run wild to insubordination, anarchy, and crime."
It was the mother at home—"the presiding genius who must
regulate all those thousand minutiae of domestic business that
demand habits of industry, order, neatness, punctuality, and
constant care"—who would determine the issue.[1]

While Beecher sought to place the home beyond the reach
of market forces, other Americans encouraged a joyous submission of the home to capitalism. The foremost advocate of
this position was Charlotte Perkins Gilman. In her 1898 volume
Women and Economics, Gilman argued for the enthusiastic acceptance of industrialized production, competitive markets, and
individualism and the elimination of homes based on the old
ways.

Feminism and Darwinism provided the philosophical framework for Gilman's work. She adopted the "gynaecocentric" thesis of the evolutionist Lester Frank Ward: that women formed

[1] Beecher, *An Essay on the Education of Female Teachers,* 67–83.

the basis of the human race and that their emancipation was "the only sure road to the evolution of man". Gilman argued, with equal bluntness, that social progress now dictated that the bond of home and economy be wholly severed. "Such affection as is maintained by economic forces", she wrote, "is not the kind which humanity needs."

In direct attack on Beecher's world of separate spheres, Gilman argued that the human species was the only animal form "in which the female depends on the male for food, the only animal species in which the sex relation is also an economic relation". This "over-development" of the "sex-distinction" caused innumerable inefficiencies, most particularly the transformation of women at home into "economic parasites". Standing in the face of economic progress, the private home was a "primitive" entity, a "clumsy tangle of rudimentary industries" that violated all the modern rules.

Fortunately, Gilman continued, the forces of social and economic change were working to undermine the position of the wife and mother in the family. The laws of capitalism — particularly the economic gain won through the specialization of labor — slated the private home for extinction, for the average homemaker was asked to be skilled in too many professions at once. "A good cook is not necessarily a good manager," she wrote, "nor a good manager an accurate and thorough cleaner, nor a good cleaner a wise purchaser." It was the savage who sought to exhibit all skills, working only for himself. The civilized human, in contrast, worked within a specialized division of labor that vastly multiplied skill, power, and output.

Already, the inexorable laws of economics had stripped the private household of many functions. By 1898, few persons still made their own candles, spun their own cloth, or cobbled their own shoes. Indeed, Gilman argued, the housekeeping functions had been reduced in most cases to only three: cleaning, cooking, and child care. The twentieth century, she added, would see these tasks also pass into the market sphere, and she devoted much of her argument to encouraging this final dismantling of the home economy. Cooking, she said, was "the lowest of amateur handicrafts and a prolific source of disease". Cleaning was handled haphazardly, still locked in practices of the preindustrial order. Turning to the nurture of children, Gilman blasted the amateurish practices of the present, arguing again that "the private home has ceased to be sufficient, or the isolated, primitive, dependent woman capable." Inadequate mothers often "murdered" their babies with poor food or "imprisoned" them in houses unhealthy even for adults. She added, "A newborn baby leads a far happier, healthier, more peaceful existence in the hands of the good trained nurse" than it did when "left on the trembling knees of the young, untrained mother".

Unlike other radicals, Gilman denied that a political revolution was necessary for this vast social change to occur. She was confident that the same forces that had industrialized other home crafts would soon undermine home-styled cleaning, cooking, and child care. Professional cleaners would offer their services, for a fee. In place of food preparation in "industrially undeveloped homes", cooking would be made efficient through rational food distribution shops, forming "large, new avenues of lucrative and honorable industry, and a new basis for human health and happiness". Housed in kitchenless homes, family members would "gradually prefer to go to their food instead of having it brought to them". Similarly, child care would be provided by businesses organized for profit and for delivering quality care through an industrial model.

Gilman was candid about the consequences of these changes. Women would be wholly liberated from the home, finally free to sell their labor for tasks to which they were individually suited. The mythology of the private home would be buried. Family bonds based on antiquated economics would disappear: "A family unity which is only bound together with a tablecloth is of questionable value." The home would no longer be "a workshop or a museum" but rather "the place of peace and rest, of love and privacy". At a deeper level, though, Gilman sought to scuttle even these qualities. A family, she said, was actually composed of "dissimilar persons"; concern about family privacy in fact prevented the "much higher and subtler forms of association" that would mark "a world of pure, strong, beautiful men and women".[2]

The third attempt to find a place for the home in the modern industrialized world was through the crafting of the new profession: home economics. In some ways, this option represented a compromise between Beecher and Gilman. Unlike Catharine Beecher, the founders of home economics fully embraced modernity, industry, and the capitalist goals of efficiency and experimentation. The "separate sphere" notion of morality was banished, and the new field explicitly sought to pull the private household into the new world of industry and efficiency. As the discipline's founding theorist, Ellen Richards, put it: "Home Economics stands for: The ideal home life of today unhampered by the traditions of the past." Unlike Gilman, though, the discipline's creators also believed that the individual home could be saved, the inherited family unit largely retained, and the woman at home retrained to fill a modernized role.

The earliest experiments in "domestic economy" date from the mid-1860s, when Vassar College implemented instruction in the household arts to complement its classical curriculum. The program of instruction took firmer root at the new landgrant colleges. In 1869, Iowa State College adopted the Holyoke plan, requiring female students to work two hours each day in the dining room, kitchen, or pantry. Three years later, the college president's wife began delivering lectures to the young women on cooking, arguing that such instruction added

---

[2] See Charlotte Perkins Gilman, *Women and Economics: A Study of the Economic Relation between Men and Women as a Factor in Social Evolution,* ed. Carl N. Degler (New York: Harper & Row, 1966 [1898]), particularly 225–317. See also Susan M. Strasser, "The Business of Housekeeping: The Ideology of the Household at the Turn of the Twentieth Century", *The Insurgent Sociologist* 7 (Fall 1978): 158–62; and Strasser, *Never Done: A History of American Housework* (New York: Pantheon Books, 1982), 219–27.

"dignity to that part of their life work hitherto considered as menial drudgery". More systematic programs followed at the universities of Kansas and Illinois. In the East, educators worried during the 1890s about the failure of many graduates of women's liberal arts colleges to marry, leading Wellesley College to offer a "house sanitation and dietetics" curriculum. Meanwhile, urban reformers opened cooking schools in New York, Boston, and other cities, designed to educate both the poor and the well-off in the applied science of food preparation.

These early experiments merged with the progressive spirit and the extraordinary American faith in education at the Lake Placid Conference on Home Economics in 1899. Ellen Richards, the first female graduate of the Massachusetts Institute of Technology, chaired the session, which marked out the boundaries of the budding profession. As the following quote reveals, concern over the apparent disintegration of the family unit dominated the meeting and helped shape the profession's self-definition. (Curiously, though, the large majority of the discipline's creators were themselves either unmarried or childless; of twenty-one "founding women", only two had ever lived simultaneously with a husband and children.[3])

> Home economics: home meaning the place of shelter and nurture for the children and for those personal qualities of self-sacrifice for others for the gaining of strength to meet the world; economics meaning the management of this home on economic lines as to time and energy as well as mere money.

On this basis, the American Home Economics Association (AHEA) organized in December 1908, with a charter membership of 700.[4]

---

[3] Noted in Strasser, "Business of Housekeeping", 149.

[4] Standard short recountings of home economics' early history are found in Earl J. McGrath and Jack T. Johnson, *The Changing Mission of Home Economics: A Report on Home Economics in the Land-Grant Colleges and State Universities* (New York: Teachers College Press, 1968), 5–16; and Olive Hall, *Home Economics Careers and Homemaking* (New York: Wiley, 1958), 27–49.

At its inception, the home economics discipline was at once traditional and modern. Traditional elements lay in the effort to craft an ideology of home life that could survive in a twentieth-century environment. The proclaimed goal was to train housewives. As Lou Allen Gregory, first professor of domestic science at the University of Illinois, explained: "It was the aim of the school to give earnest and capable young women a liberal and practical education, which should fit them for their great duties and trusts, making them the equals of their educated husbands." Julia Lathrop, first head of the U.S. Children's Bureau, encouraged housekeepers to "study their families and their children" and thought that the "profession of carrying on households" would be "constantly stimulated by research" at the universities. [5]

As an expression of economic modernity, home economics marked the transition of households from productive to consuming units. Beyond the ritual sewing classes, relatively little attention was given to retraining girls in productive activities. Rather, the focus was on educated consumption, a thorough merging of the home sphere with the industrial sphere, and the retooling of the homemaker as a purchasing agent. With the experimental efficiencies of "Taylorism" the vogue among progressive corporations, home economists also sought to translate the principles of time-motion studies and "one best way" for household tasks. In her popular books *The New Housekeeping* (1919), *Household Engineering: Scientific Management in the Home* (1920), and *Selling Mrs. Consumer* (1929), Christine Frederick created the career of "household engineer", based on a study of factory systems and the use of her own home as an "experiment station". Frederick's basic principle was scheduling: "Plan what you are going to do, do it, and then rest." The homemaker was both executive and manual laborer (in fact, a situation

---

[5] Quoted in Isabel Bevier and Susannah Usher, *The Home Economics Movement* (Boston: Whitcomb & Barrons, 1906), 31; and Julia Lathrop, "The Family", lecture given Feb. 8, 1916; quoted in Strasser, *Never Done,* 209.

wholly at odds with Taylorism), and "the more management" a woman put into housework, "the less friction and the less nervous energy she will have to expend". Careful meal planning, the efficient grouping of kitchen equipment, extensive household records, and a rigorous family budget formed specific tasks.

Yet Frederick's purpose in saving time and effort was linked "to the attainment of the higher ends of personal and family happiness and success". With leisure time, the housewife could study to improve her skills, learn more about her husband's business, more closely supervise her children's work or play, or improve her mental life. Moreover, Frederick was resolutely opposed to paid labor for wives. "Our greatest enemy is the woman with the career", she wrote in the *Journal of Home Economics*. She called on the married woman with a job to return home and discover that it is "just as interesting to care for her own children as it is to go down on the east side and take care of Annie Bolowski".[6]

When the new discipline became the favored child of the federal government, job opportunities multiplied. In an attempt by progressives to save both the family farm and the family, Congress passed the Smith–Lever Act of 1914 "to aid in diffusing among the people of the United States useful and practical information on the subjects relating to agriculture and home economics". The law created the Cooperative Extension Service and a new rural constituency for the home economics profession, which would dominate it through World War II. The Vocational Education Act followed in 1917, providing federal funds to pay the salaries of home economics teachers. Predictably, the number of such teachers climbed dramatically, and by 1920 six thousand U.S. high schools offered home economics courses. Twenty years later, virtually all American high

---

[6] See Christine Frederick, *Household Engineering: Scientific Management in the Home* (Chicago: American School of Home Economics, 1920); *Selling Mrs. Consumer* (New York: The Business Course, 1929); and "Points of Efficiency", *Journal of Home Economics* (hereafter *JHE*) 6 (June 1914): 280.

schools, rural and urban, placed girls in such classes. Accordingly, university-based schools of home economics shifted their focus to teacher training. The Great Depression and World War II reinforced the discipline's original emphasis on food, clothing, and shelter.[7]

Following the war, though, this "stitch and stir" orientation began troubling leaders in the field, and they worked to expand the profession's self-definition to embrace "human relations" and psychology. In the short run, this extension of purpose appeared to intensify the discipline's family orientation. The goal of the AHEA, as related in 1953, was "the attainment of the well-being of individuals and of families, the improvement of homes, and the preservation of values significant in home life". Members of the profession still celebrated the position of homemaker as "the largest single occupation of college women graduates" and emphasized the importance of the college "home ec" major in preparing the student "for homemaking rather than for a wage-earning profession". Textbooks praised homemakers who dedicated "both their reason and emotion to their high calling", who were resourceful in outlook, who coupled "constructive imagination" with "executive ability", and who possessed "a genuine desire to be of service to others". Indeed, wage-earning careers were denigrated; the home elevated. As UCLA's Olive Hall wrote in 1955, women's "greatest fulfillment comes through their own home and family. The home is truly the center of a woman's life. . . . [The homemaker] knows that she is performing a task that is the very pivot of society." Swollen enrollment figures at the universities in the 1950s gave numerical support to this enthusiasm.[8]

Yet this embrace of psychological goals also subtly shifted

[7] On the entry of government into home economics, see Strasser, *Never Done,* 225–35; and McGrath and Johnson, *Changing Mission of Home Economics,* 11–13.

[8] Hall, *Home Economics Careers,* 38, 77–84; and Selma F. Lippeatt and Helen I. Brown, *Focus and Promise of Home Economics: A Family-Oriented Perspective* (New York: Macmillan, 1965), 89ff.

emphasis from family integrity to personal fulfillment and the "companionate marriage". In "New Directions: A Statement of Philosophy and Objectives", adopted in 1959, the AHEA assumed "a unique responsibility for helping girls and boys, women and men, to achieve wholesome, happy lives". Helen LeBaron, dean of Iowa State University's School of Home Economics, argued in 1955 that the discipline must refocus its attention "on a study of *problems of the family,* irrespective of the subject matter thus affected". Michigan State's Anna Creekmore praised the profession's growing deemphasis on "the material culture surrounding the homemaker and her household" and the new attention given "to the family in the home situation, with the social wellbeing of all members the major concern". [9]

This change of direction and slight loss of self-confidence during the late 1950s turned into a more far-reaching crisis during the next decade. By 1968, one observer described home economics as in "turmoil", marked by "general confusion about what we're doing", and "a frantic search for identity and status". The immediate institutional concern was the place of the discipline in the burgeoning modern research universities. As two prominent educators noted, home economics in the land-grant schools "was fractured with disputes about its function and its future. Was it merely a collection of disparate specialties, or did it have a distinctive and unifying core? What research should it include, and how should such research be organized?" [10]

The discipline's theorists began a frantic look for a more scientific core. One writer proposed scuttling any reference at

[9] Committee on Philosophy and Objectives of Home Economics, American Home Economics Association, *Home Economics' New Directions: A Statement of Philosophy and Objectives* (Washington, DC: AHEA, 1959), 5; Helen R. LeBaron, "Home Economics — Its Potential for Greater Service", *JHE* 47 (Sept. 1955): 468–69; and Anna Creekmore, "The Concept Basic to Home Economics", *JHE* 60 (Feb. 1968): 94.

[10] Creekmore, "Concept Basic to Home Economics", 93; McGrath and Johnson, *Changing Mission of Home Economics*, 16.

all to homemaking and family, embracing instead the waxing interest in environmentalism. As a definition of purpose, she proposed "home economics as the study of man as a total being, his near environment, and the interaction between them". More useful, it turned out, was the theoretical emphasis on "family problems", specifically "the overpopulation crisis". With an enthusiasm born of desperation, the AHEA embraced population control in the late 1960s as "one of the Association's most vital concerns". Partly stimulated by a major grant from the U.S. Agency for International Development (another sign of the profession's dependence on federal largesse), home economists turned their energies to reducing the number of American children and endorsed state "population education" programs, abortion on demand, delayed marriage, and voluntary childlessness.[11]

Some continuity with old themes remained. As late as 1968, the AHEA's journal was still running an occasional article on homemaking, such as "Procedures and Temperatures for Roasting Chicken". Then came the feminist challenge, and home economics — the supposed disciplined defender of the modern homemaker and her family — collapsed, utterly and completely.

Signs of the revival of individualist or liberal feminism began seeping into AHEA publications in the mid-1960s. Between 1968 and 1972, the subject came to dominate professional concern. The early shifts included a subtle devaluation of the housewife's contribution. Writing in 1968, a Rutgers University home economist urged colleagues to discourage students from viewing homemaking as a lifetime career. Instead, young women should be taught "the importance of gainful employment" and techniques for selecting day care, and both young men and women should learn that two incomes would probably be

[11] Creekmore, "Concept Basic to Home Economics", 95; Katherine B. Oettinger, "Family Planning: A Critical Issue", *JHE* 61 (Oct. 1969): 609–10; "Resolutions from the 1971 Annual Meeting on Abortion and the Status of Women", *JHE* 63 (Sept. 1971): 473; and "The Time Is Now: AHEA Resolutions on Population", *JHE* 64 (Sept. 1972): 35.

necessary for an adequate standard of living.[12] More blunt was Francesca Miller's article "Womanpower". The United States, she stated, had failed "to create a caring society" that was "dedicated to human concerns". To correct this, the necessary first step was to end "women's continued imprisonment in domesticity". Home economists had been too successful in training students to believe that "the family is important". In the contemporary social crisis, the family must now give way to "the community".[13]

Such sentiments quickly grew into a sustained chant. At the AHEA's 1970 convention, sociologist Jessie Bernard emphasized the need to encourage childlessness among students. Marriage, too, was "really not all that good for women". The private household was an unnatural phenomenon. Families were "excess baggage". The 1950s — an era "when women felt they had to go home and have babies, bake bread, and weave in order to be a woman" — were the "Lost Decade". Home economist Roslyn Willett agreed that the domesticity of that period was "a curious low point" for women. The nation now needed fewer private homes and fewer mothers, since "mother love in the suburbs too often tends to be 'smother' love." Iowa Sate's Helen Hilton argued that traditional homemakers had been "brainwashed" by the culture in which they were raised, that the family had perpetuated the inferior status of women, and that home economists must reeducate themselves to the feminist agenda. Penn State's Marjorie East described, in glowing terms, the family of the year 2000, a wonderfully "socialized, interdependent world" where girls would be inoculated against ovulation at age 10, where the bearing of a child would be licensed and rigidly controlled, where the care of infants would "not be left to the haphazard and amateurish efforts of parents" but would "be carried out by experts", where society would "not want

[12] Mary B. Kievil, "Women in Gainful and Useful Employment", *JHE* 60 (Nov. 1968): 701–2.
[13] Francesca L. Miller, "Womanpower: Rediscovering a Prime Resource", *JHE* 60 (Nov. 1968): 695–96.

any drones called 'housewives'". East added that she and her colleagues were already designing a new home economics curriculum "that will secure these blessings for posterity".[14]

While the profession, in a figurative sense, thus began to sow the seeds of its destruction, a few voices still urged self-interested reason. At the 1970 AHEA convention, Catherine Chilman of Hood College warned that as ever more women earned their living outside their homes, "they are becoming, in fact, detrained for daily domesticity." Similarly, hysteria over the supposed population crisis left women "apologetic" about having babies and motherhood denuded of honor.[15]

Then came Robin Morgan, editor of *Sisterhood Is Powerful,* and such dissenting voices were effectively silenced. In an address to the 1972 AHEA convention, Morgan laid the matter squarely on the line. The main emphasis of their organization, she reminded the delegates, was "to reinforce three primary areas: marriage, the family, and the issue of consumerism. . . . Now those three areas . . . [are] the primary areas that the radical women's movement is out to destroy. So one could say that as a radical feminist, I am here addressing the enemy." Morgan charged that young women who passed through home economics courses were usually left as "a limp, jibbering mass of jelly waiting for marriage". Indeed, by feminist standards, home economics was so corrupt in its nature that the speaker had only one unambiguous recommendation: "You can quit your jobs." For those who must stay on, she urged that they work to eliminate the home economics requirement for junior and senior high school women and impose it instead on high school men. Home economists should also "tell people the truth" about

[14] Jessie Bernard and Catherine Chiman, "Changing Lifestyles for Women: Their Significance to Families", *JHE* 62 (Oct. 1970): 575–77, 581–82; Roslyn Willett, "Do Not Stereotype Women", *JHE* 63 (Oct. 1971): 549–51; Helen LeBaron Hilton, "Now That Women Are Liberated", *JHE* 64 (April 1972): 3–5; and Marjorie East, "Family Life in the Year 2000", *JHE* 62 (Jan. 1970): 13–18.

[15] Bernard and Chilman, "Changing Lifestyles for Women", 577.

the housewife's role and "the despair she faces in her life" and "about the economic bigotry against women". Above all, those who stayed in the obsolete profession must work to "change" social mores, not reinforce them. Home economics was "hooked" into institutions that were "dying". Morgan concluded: "It's your choice whether you're going to crumble with that system . . . while history rolls over you or whether you're going to move with [history]. I hope that you will join us—but we're going to win in any event." [16]

AHEA's leadership moved quickly to join, en masse, the course of history and so reverse the founding purposes of their profession. The organization created the Women's Role Committee, which soon intoned the expected platitudes. Home economics "was part of the problem rather than a solution". Efforts must be made to ensure that happy homemakers not contaminate the ambitions of career women. Traditional high school teachers needed to be retrained as advocates of alternative lifestyles and gender-role engineering. "It's very necessary to get to the boys in high school" and teach them to stitch and stir and about "the changing roles of men and women". In all, Morgan's speech "was good for the Association because she really did stir us up and made us take a second look at what we were doing". [17]

A crescendo of "reorientation" was quickly reached. According to a home economist from the University of Tennessee, the provision of "unisex experiences for all children so as to free them from the rigid mold of previous stereotypes" must speedily begin. Their discipline, she added, was the unit "best able" to conduct research on gender roles and so become an important branch of "women's studies". "Scholars" began to eliminate sex roles "arbitrarily assigned to one sex rather than the other" from home economics textbooks. Others worked

[16] "What Robin Morgan Said in Denver", *JHE* 65 (Jan. 1973): 13.
[17] "The Women's Role Committee Speaks Out", *JHE* 65 (Jan. 1973): 10–12, 14–15.

to suppress the maternal instinct. Noting that teenage girls wanted more children than boys and that young people were still partially socialized for marital roles, writers urged efforts to "free" students to make other choices. "Alternative life styles" should be encouraged, and "values ought to be freely chosen".[18]

Even before the "revolution" had reached full steam, its impact on youthful imaginations was already evident. Interviews with teenage members of Future Homemakers of America (an organization then jointly sponsored by the AHEA and the U.S. Office of Education) revealed confused young girls, committed in their hearts to marriage and children but taught by their instructors to forget the joys of family life. "I plan to bear no children as I feel there are too many unwanted babies", said one respondent. "Why have several children when the world is already overpopulated?" said another. The young home-makers-to-be also stressed that "children should feel they are equals" to their parents and that the only legitimate goal left to them was "a busy career life", complete with quality day care and frequent family meals outside the home.[19]

This scenario, of course, is precisely the vision laid out by Charlotte Perkins Gilman eighty years before. With their words, the future homemakers declared her victory over the rival creators of the discipline of home economics. Indeed, as historian Susan Strasser has emphasized, recent events have elevated Gilman into "the best prophet of her time".[20] In a period dominated by KinderCare, McDonald's, Merry Maid Cleaners, and the web of child protection agencies, home life approached full industrialization, and the "science" of homemaking was vanishing.

[18] See L. B. Celik, "Women's Studies and Home Economics", *JHE* 67 (Jan. 1975): 29–30; Sandra S. Hutton, "Sex Role Illustrations in Junior High School Home Economics Textbooks", *JHE* 68 (March 1976): 27–30; and Anne Johnson, "Teaching Population Education to Home Economics Students", *JHE* 66 (Nov. 1974): 10–13.

[19] "How Does Youth Envision the 1984 Family?" *JHE* 64 (Nov. 1972): 20–24.

[20] Strasser, *Never Done,* 219.

The irony in this is that just as home economists left the barricades, gave up the battle, and embraced the opposition, researchers in a very different discipline were beginning to understand and document the vital social and economic role that had been played by the modern "homemaker" in holding the most corrosive of capitalism's incentives at bay.

The needed breakthrough in analytical economics came in a 1965 article by Gary Becker of the University of Chicago. [21] In prior decades, economic analysis of the household had been stymied by the problem of "unexplained variations in tastes", which prevented the explanation or prediction of behavior. In breaking the deadlock, Becker offered a simple insight: "Time is money." Personal decisions on the use of leisure ("nonmarket") time and on choice of a marriage mate, family size, divorce, or "life style" were all susceptible to economic analysis, once one understood that these choices involved the allocation of scarce resources (including "psychic income" such as love) among competing ends. [22]

Appropriately, this mode of analysis was soon called "the new home economics", and it began to produce important insights about the place of gender roles and the homemaker in the economy. Researchers discovered, for example, that the professional education of women was significantly related to family formation. Additional years spent by women in training for paid employment resulted in later marriages and a growing tendency to avoid the altar altogether. [23] Others noted that whereas a marriage between a working man and a woman at home made valuable economic sense (each bringing complementary skills to the marital bond so that both are "better off" than if they remained single), a marriage between economic

[21] Gary S. Becker, "A Theory of the Allocation of Time", *Economic Journal* 75 (1965): 493–517.

[22] See Robert T. Michael and Gary Becker, "On the New Theory of Consumer Behavior", *Swedish Journal of Economics* 75 (1973): 379–96.

[23] Michael C. Keeley, "The Economics of Family Formation", *Economic Inquiry* 15 (April 1977): 247.

equals offered less direct gain, since the true "division of labor" in a household was thereby sacrificed. This meant that "risk adverse" individuals will tend to rely more on "trial marriages". Existing marriages, moreover, will tend to be more fragile and divorce increasingly popular.[24]

In analyzing recent fertility trends, the new home economists say that the replacement of the homemaker by the career-oriented women drives birthrates ever downward. In a 1979 study, researchers showed that two variables largely account for fertility trends in the United States since 1945: fathers' income, which varies directly with fertility (more money means more births), and the "opportunity costs" of women, which vary inversely with fertility (rising real wages and employment opportunities for women mean ever-fewer births). Accordingly, in a society where traditional families — male wage earner and female homemaker — predominate, economic growth will stimulate fertility. However, in a society in which women's job opportunities are expanding and their potential pay moving toward equality with men's, economic growth will drive fertility downward, with no apparent stopping point. For example, the "baby boom" of the 1945–62 era was also a period when cultural norms reinforced the homemaker role, male wages rose steadily, and the real wages of American women rose very slightly. By way of contrast, the "baby bust" of the 1960s and 1970s occurred during a period when the homemaker and mother were denigrated, when equal opportunity laws opened new career paths for women, and when the average hourly wage for women soared. In short, the "new home economics" shows that America has entered a new social-economic era in which an increase in real per capita gross national product results in a decline in fertility. Indeed, the "more equal" men and women become in job opportunities and wage scales and

[24] See John Ermisch, "Investigation into the Causes of the Postwar Fertility Swings", in *Population Change and Social Planning,* ed., David Eversley and Wolfgang Kollmann (London: Edward Arnold, 1982), 144–51.

the more rapid the economic expansion, the more will fertility move toward zero. [25]

So, in the end it appears that the scientific "homemaker" was not just an arbitrary or perverse status designed to suppress women. Rather, she was, in a very real sense, the "pivot" of industrial society, an artificially created social role that managed for a time to reconcile industrial capitalism with the family, that allowed for human reproduction within a system of sustained economic growth. With the majority of American women in the homemaking role during their child-rearing years, as was the case as late as the 1950s, Americans could have both economic growth and their children. With the number of purposeful homemakers now dwindling, Americans face the steady disappearance of children.

Charlotte Gilman had, in a way, foreseen the problem, noting that the movement of all women into the paid labor force would result in fewer births. Yet she had turned to Darwin to resolve the issue: "If women did choose professions unsuitable to maternity, Nature would quietly extinguish them by her unvarying process." [26] What if the development proved to be almost universally true? Gilman had no answer.

Might it be possible to restore a true "home economics" to its pristine middle way? Unfortunately, the collapse of the discipline in the face of liberal feminism was probably preordained. By bringing the methods and the logic of industry into the home, home economists set in motion processes that must eventually result in the disappearance of the autonomous family. For the family is, broadly speaking, precapitalistic, based on communitarian rather than individualistic principles and resting

[25] See William P. Butz and Michael P. Ward, "Will U.S. Fertility Remain Low? A New Economic Interpretation", *Population and Development Review* 5 (Dec. 1979): 663–83; and Robert J. Willis, "A New Approach to the Economic Theory of Fertility Behavior", *Journal of Political Economy* 81 (March–April 1973): S14–S69.

[26] Gilman, *Women and Economics,* 246.

on ideals such as sharing, self-sacrifice, and altruism. The pursuit of efficiency, useful in building automobiles, very quickly becomes corrosive inside premodern structures such as the home, undermining the very system it was intended to save. A "middle way" could not be sustained. The modern role of "homemaker", despite the best efforts of its enthusiasts, could not hold back the tide.

Seven

An Elusive Harmony

These varied American experiments in family preservation in the industrial age powerfully converged in the 1945–65 period. Although direct wage discrimination in favor of male households was in retreat, the informal family wage—codified through cultural assumptions about "male" and "female" jobs—grew in prominence and in its ability to alter the wage system in a family-supportive manner. At the same time, the American suburban environment enjoyed its most rapid expansion, as young couples poured into the new communities. Among all the major American denominations, religious faith seemed to exhibit again a family-centered core, with a particularly strong display among Roman Catholics. The American experiment in a nationalistic welfare state, resting on a sense of solidarity, also enjoyed its fullest blossoming in this period of Cold War. Meanwhile, enrollment in home economics courses reached new highs in the continuing effort to tame the industrial impulse within the family.

For a time, there was impressive statistical evidence suggesting that, under these influences, a new balance had been found. The American birthrate recovered from Depression-era lows and climbed to a level unseen since World War I. Most surprisingly, college-educated women were in the vanguard of this recovery, with their fertility more than doubling. The creation of new family households proceeded at a record pace, and the proportion of Americans living in married-couple households with children reached another historical high. Between 1947 and 1960, the divorce rate reversed a hundred-year trend and steadily declined. The average age of first marriage fell below 21 for women, another unprecedented figure, and these same women embraced domesticity and homemaking with purposeful commitment. The schools overflowed with children, and America seemed once again to be a youthful, child-centered, family-oriented land.

Yet the social euphoria and apparent family strength of the 1950s quickly unraveled in the 1965–80 era. These experiments in family solidarity showed stress and decline at the same time that statistical measures of family health turned negative. The family wage concept, the housing bias in favor of families, distinctively religious family behavior, a traditionalist military socialism, and a self-confident home economics all vanished or fell into disarray. Meanwhile, the birthrate tumbled sharply after 1962. Ten years later, the U.S. total fertility rate fell to the "replacement" level — that is, each generation just manages to reproduce itself. By 1976, U.S. fertility was 15 percent below that zero-growth figure. The divorce rate climbed 150 percent in the same period, while the proportion of births outside of wedlock soared. The suburbs grew gray, and the sense of new community began to sour. By the mid-1970s, a growing body of American women viewed domesticity as a trap and looked to market labor and careers as their priorities.

On the one hand, it could be argued that these results were not economically preordained: that the restored family-centered world of the 1950s might have survived indefinitely, but for a shift in dominant thinking and willful action. Put another way, ideas and other noneconomic externalities were the driving force for change, an interpretation backed by some evidence. Certainly, the assaults on the informal social constitution of the United States, starting in the mid-nineteenth century, were heavily driven by ideology and politics. The crafting of the *parens patriae* doctrine in 1839, to choose one early example, was a judicial power grab unrelated to economic circumstances, but one with baleful long-term consequences for American families. Similarly, the steady surrender of the Tenth Amendment of the U.S. Constitution to the Fourteenth Amendment could have been forestalled by a more aggressive political defense of the authentic federal principle. Bolstering this case, the family wage system in America actually grew in strength and popularity through 1940. Direct challenges to its existence and justice by manufacturers and individualist feminists had been turned back as recently as the 1920s. From this perspective, it was mobilization for total war in the 1940s and the complete triumph of liberal feminism over social feminism in the 1960s that put an end to the family wage ideal.

Expanding on the argument, one might attribute the failure of both the suburban strategy and the religious possibility to a slippage of standards. Federal officials, for example, subtly but deliberately shifted their emphasis in housing from traditional father-headed families to a less normative approach, and reallocated their subsidies accordingly. Among American Catholics, steadfastness in doctrine on the family during the 1950s gave way to debate and confusion in the 1960s, which arguably undermined the distinctive "Catholic fertility". Clearer moral leadership in either case, it could be argued, would have sustained traditional family living through the 1960s and beyond. The military's family orientation of the Cold War, similarly, might have continued indefinitely, but for the loss of national confidence and will in the Vietnam ordeal. In all cases, new profamily social and political agendas would naturally aim at recovering the family framework of the remarkable 1950s.

On the other hand, such arguments may underestimate the unique and continuing effects of industrial organization on society, and the sustained pressures on family living brought by the union of mega-corporations and bureaucracy. Karl Polanyi's analysis of the "Great Transformation" offers a more sobering and convincing account of many of these changes. Concerning work, he argues that the triumphant principle of freedom of contract meant perpetual challenges to the noncontractual arrangements of kinship, neighborhood, profession, and religious belief. "To separate labor from other activities of life", Polanyi writes, "and to subject it to the laws of the market was to annihilate all organic forms of existence and to replace them by a different type of organization, an atomistic and individual-

istic one." This "commoditization" of labor was complemented
by a commercialization of the soil, with related consequences:
"To detach man from the soil meant the dissolution of the body
economic into its elements so that each element could fit into
that part of the system where it was most useful."[1] The contemporary phrase "work station" properly captures the atomized
nature of modern human labor.

Writing in 1920, G. K. Chesterton saw the same peril. While
describing in detail the ruin of families through "the coercive
spirit of the state", he concluded that "an even more ferocious
enemy of the family is the factory." He continued:

> [The family] is literally being torn in pieces, in that the hus-
> band may go to one factory, the wife to another, and the child
> to a third. Each will become the servant of a separate financial
> group, which is more and more gaining the political power of
> a feudal group. But whereas feudalism received the loyalty of
> families, the lords of the new servile state will receive only the
> loyalty of individuals; that is, of lonely men and even of lost
> children.[2]

The varied efforts over the last 150 years to rebuild a basis
for family life in America derived from a common recognition
of these systemic pressures. Those projects that succeeded for
a time—such as the culturally imposed family wage system—
did so only as long as their partisans understood the root problem, continuously shored up their response, and avoided the
fatal temptation of using state authority to achieve their ends.
Such systems also rested on a societywide willingness to live
with the short-term costs generated by a somewhat inefficient
distribution of human labor. However, when the defenders of
family integrity grew uncertain, lost heart, rejected the necessary costs, relied on state power for aid or protection, or lost
the needed sense of proportion, these barriers to atomistic eco-

---

[1] Polanyi, *Great Transformation,* 163, 179.

[2] G. K. Chesterton, *The Superstition of Divorce,* in *Collected Works.* Vol. IV.
Family, Society, Politics (San Francisco: Ignatius Press, 1987), 259–60.

nomic and political incentives disappeared, and family life weakened.

This interpretation presupposes that the biological family is a premodern entity, necessarily organized on nonmarket principles. Indeed, it sees the family as the social unit — the "cell of society" — that alone can successfully embody the socialist principle: "from each according to his ability, to each according to his need". Family life survives only as the members of this small community defy, through tradition or intention, the incentives or pressures that would transform all human actions into market exchanges or subsume them to globalist economic goals. When the family structure surrenders to market organization, it disappears as a meaningful entity with the power to hold or shield its members from the depredations of rival centers of authority.

This perspective acknowledges that markets deliver the highest quality goods and services to the most people at the cheapest price, which is capitalism's strongest claim, even its glory. Yet it also presupposes that human existence must mean more than efficient production and consumption. Successful communities — ranging from families to nations — are those that build barriers to market pressures around certain institutions, such as the family, and channel other behaviors so as to place limits on the secular incentives of the market. Long experience would suggest that cultural, rather than political, structures are the only ones effective in these crucial societal tasks. For example, whereas the "state imposed" family wage, consisting of legal minimum wages differentiated by gender, actually produced results that ran counter to intent, the cultural "family wage", resting on "male" and "female" job categories, could, if judged on its own terms, claim success. Similarly, culturally determined biases among FHA underwriters had a strong influence over their decisions on housing mortgages, independent of the written law, which for a time helped sustain a renewed family system. Both projects, though, survived only as long as cultural bias trumped the egalitarian leveling of both the marketplace and the state. Building on this interpretation, a profamily agenda would rest primarily on cultural efforts to prohibit the entry of market incentives into key areas of social life.

Are there more specific lessons to be drawn from these American struggles over the divorce of home from work? First, and most important, the autonomous family is endangered by both unchanneled market forces *and* state authority. These two abstractions — the capitalist market and modern government — have a common interest in the decomposition of the family unit into its constituent parts: parents and children; males and females; old and young; mothers and infants. In every case of family decline, the market economy gains independent economic actors who can be reorganized with individuals from other weakened families into more efficient production units. Similarly, the state apparatus gains both taxable income and potential dependents, as newly "free" individuals look for a measure of social security to replace the protections once afforded by family. The great error of many family defenders has been their eager turn to state coercive authority as a means of defending the family and tradition from the capitalist market. The common result has been a further diminishing of the autonomous family. Indeed, family units rarely face greater danger than when large corporations *and* government combine in an effort to "help" them: such exercises in state capitalism will in fact bury the family in a grave full of warm sentiment.

A second lesson is that religion, or religious belief, cannot function as a substitute economy. The failure of "Catholic fertility" in the late 1960s was more than a reaction to doctrinal confusion. The evidence suggests that in the social and political maelstrom of the 1965–75 period, Catholic couples simply grew weary of their biological burden and brought an end to their heroic defiance of the economic incentives. To its credit, the Papacy in the industrial era has consistently understood that religious devotion would never be sufficient to ensure a rightly ordered world. Its search, by fits and starts, for a "third eco-

nomic way" reflects this perceived need for a material economy compatible with received doctrine.[3] The apparent end to
"Mormon exceptionalism" in the 1980s supports the same conclusion. Although teachings on family living by church leaders
remained faithful and strong, Mormon couples appear to have
succumbed to the common pressures of an industrialized economy, particularly mounting demand for the labor of married
women, and to a welfare state that discourages large families.
Their biological defiance of economic incentives for religious
ends eventually gave in to the late-twentieth-century realities
of males' stagnant real wages, mounting taxes, the socialization of children's time and insurance value, and the leveling
of gender roles.

A third lesson is that a nationalistic welfare state in America
centered on the "Cold War family" succeeded only briefly and
under circumstances unlikely to be repeated. To begin with,
the United States of the 1945–65 period existed in an environment of perceived external danger, with communism cast as
a fundamental challenge to American interests, which created
a strong incentive toward internal conformity. The United
States was also, in ethnic terms, unusually stable at this time.
Massive immigration into America had been choked off by con-
gressional acts in 1921 and 1924. By the late 1940s, virtually
all citizens were at least one generation removed from the im-
migrant experience and unusually committed to a generic
Americanism. Although tensions between blacks and whites
certainly remained, and would later grow, the 1950s were
surprisingly stable in ethnic terms and generated — however
briefly — a measure of the "solidarity" that has always been
found at the heart of the more homogeneous, more sweeping,
and more successful Scandinavian welfare states. With the Immigration Act of 1965, though, the United States entered a

---

[3] For a brief history and a recent version of this, see Carl A. Anderson and
William J. Gribbin, *The Family in the Modern World: A Symposium on Pope John
Paul II's Familiaris Consortio* (Washington, DC: American Family Institute, 1982).

radically different phase of national development, creating a new ethnic diversity and a consequent splintering of values and the sense of shared experience, which seem to defy all efforts at rebuilding cohesion.

A fourth lesson is that the widely analyzed and much praised companionate family, rooted in shared consumption and emotional support, failed as a meaningful focus of American loyalty and as a bulwark against both the ambitions of government and the atomistic incentives of the economy. Building family life on the companionate model was the great error of the suburban enthusiasts of the 1950s. They believed that emotion alone could sustain a home life that institutionalized the separation of men's labor from family living and left women in their houses as professionalized child and home managers. Yet this vision ultimately faltered, as seen in the progressive dissolution of companionate family bonds in the decades after 1960.

A fifth lesson is the false promise of current family saving strategies. In recent years, the preferred strategy to accommodate the divorce of family from work has become family reorganization through public policy changes to meet the full industrialization of social life. Specifics include greater public subsidies for day-care and early childhood development programs, the provision of generous parental leaves by employers and the state to new parents, government-guaranteed health insurance for women and children, job sharing, and enhanced part-time work.[4] Yet underneath its profamily veneer, this approach is simply a reworking of the Gilman plan, stripped of its more extreme rhetoric and still lodged in the family-consuming power of the corporate state. Families are "valued", to

[4] See, recently, Sylvia Ann Hewlett, "Good News? The Private Sector and Win-Win Scenarios", and Edward F. Zigler and Elizabeth P. Gilman, "An Agenda for the 1990's: Supporting Families", in *Rebuilding the Nest: A New Commitment to the American Family,* ed. David Blankenhorn, Steven Bayme, and Jean Bethke Elshtain (Milwaukee, WI: Family Service America, 1990), 207–26, 237–49.

be sure, but only as they surrender autonomy and conform either to industrial organization or to a form of state control, so giving up their "family" nature.

Another program for the reconciliation of work and home looks to recent technological changes that suggest a historic resolution of the family-work dilemma. The term *postindustrial* has been often used and abused and sometimes means little more than the loss of competitive advantage relative to other nations. Yet some commentators see real signs that, although centralization in factory and office has been the guiding concept for 150 years of economic change, decentralization may be a better guide in the decades ahead. They argue that new computer and communication technologies will bring work home again. Or they cite the new availability of computer hardware and software as the necessary bases for creating successful home schools, a specialized version of home production. Why bind the American family to the industrial metaphor after a century and a half of efforts to avoid that fate, especially since the metaphor itself shows signs of obsolescence?[5]

In practice, though, the promised technological rescue of family life rarely materializes. Experiments in telecommunicating between home and central office have, so far, had mixed results, and have yet to make a statistical dent. Similarly, home-based entrepreneurial ventures carry all of the risks normally associated with small businesses and report the same high casualty rate, a fate usually rooted in undercapitalization. Moreover, home schooling exacts a high structural, emotional, and financial price among families so engaged, costs rarely affected by the available electronic gimmickry.

In the end, there are no easy, indirect solutions to the dilemma of the family in industrial society. Mankind cannot escape the dictates of its biological nature and the innate drive for a stable

---

[5] Among the techno-enthusiasts are Alvin Toffler, *Future Shock* (New York: Random House, 1970), and John Naisbitt, *Megatrends: Ten New Directions Transforming Our Lives* (New York: Warner Books, 1982).

life within a family. Nor can it permanently tame the revolutionary thrust of industrial capitalism through state power without putting itself at even greater risk. Nor is love enough to hold a family together. The family's survival as an autonomous unit still requires that love and intimacy be concretely expressed through a common economic life of both production and consumption. Meaningful family survival depends on the building and maintenance of a true household economy, one that exists apart from the national and international economies and that reconciles the claims of the dependent young, old, and sick with the abilities and obligations of those able to work. Toward these ends, both men and women are still called home to relearn and recommit to the deeper meanings of the ancient words *husbandry* and *housewifery*.

In consequence, the core requirements of family reconstruction are, at once, reactionary and radical, involving the recovery of human character and immediate community. The American republic presupposed the necessary character type: persons who cherish their economic autonomy, rooted in stable families and the possession of land and property. The broader elements of the necessary social structure have long been understood. The needed "ideal type" was ably described by sociologist Carle Zimmerman in his classic book *Family and Society*. In his search for a guide to "family reconstruction", Zimmerman analyzed in depth "a simple but relatively prosperous family" living in the American heartland. This family "has sufficient food, clothing, and shelter for all basic needs", although its members "have little money from our commercial standards and purchase few goods". It is "strongly familistic", he continued, and "highly integrated. . . . [T]hey observe local customs rigidly. The home and the hearth are the center of their familistic enterprises." Powerful moral and religious codes govern this family form, reinforcing "regular habits of work", obedience to parents, and thrift. Although this family "contributes little to the agriculture surplus of the nation", none of its members are "a burden on the relief funds of country, state, or federal agencies. On the contrary, it stands ready to help its absent members."

Other basic functions reside in this social unit. "The family hearth is supplemented by the work of the school, so that the education of the child remains home-centered." As they grow into adulthood, children benefit from the setting in other ways: "They receive capital with which to start, and a good name in the community." Their family-centered economy also bonds well to their place: "The soil assures good returns in products for the labor expended. The climate and the rainfall are sufficiently beneficent to permit normal growing seasons." In this setting, Zimmerman reported, family life thrives amidst the upheavals of prosperity and recession.[6]

Using a term adopted from LePlay, Zimmerman labeled this social form a "stem family". Most importantly, he insisted that this family model was not an expression of some dying or transitional past. Rather, Zimmerman marshaled evidence to show that it was a pattern recurring at various times and places in history. Indeed, he insisted that the "stem family" was, in practice, optional for every age. It develops, Zimmerman said, "among all people who combine the benefits of agriculture, industry, and settled life with the common sense idea of defending their private life from the domination of legislators, from the invasion of bureaucrats, and from the exaggerations of the manufacturing regime".[7] Its root requirement was and is a people of character, sustained by faith and guided by a love of liberty, who understand the intertwined perils of materialism and oppression.

Chesterton described the task in more graphic form. From its first days in the forest, he wrote, the family had to fight against wild monsters, "and so it is now fighting against these wild machines. It only managed to survive then, and it will only manage to survive now, by a strong internal sanctity; a

[6] Zimmerman and Framptom, *Family and Society,* 221–37.
[7] Ibid., 133.

tacit oath or dedication deeper than that of the city or the tribe."[8]

Development of a people and society in this way would begin with a focus on personal character and move toward a broadened distribution of land and other private property among the citizens, with a strong preference for family-held and -operated enterprises. Hilaire Belloc, the Vanderbilt Agrarians, and Wendell Berry have, in different times and places, joined with Chesterton and Zimmerman in offering a shared vision of the good society, reborn through a primary commitment to autonomous families rooted in communities of character.[9] The very success of American groups living in this milieu, such as the Amish and the Hutterites, testifies to the practical truth of Zimmerman's observation about their ability to survive, and even prosper, in any age, while their very peculiarity highlights the enormity — some would say the impossibility — of the challenge.

In the 1990s, to be sure, the modern system of state capitalism, combining personal liberation from traditional ties and an obsession with equalitarianism with an economy predicated on mass consumption and a common dependence on the welfare state, has no meaningful rivals. Rather than a return to natural human community, the more predictable future is another round of futile social and political engineering in which Americans will continue their elusive quest for an artificial harmony between the domain of modern industry and the domain of nurture and reproduction. Failing societywide renewal, families may, of necessity, fall back on the more modest, but more perilous, strategy of simply protecting their small communities

[8] Chesterton, *Collected Works,* Vol. IV, 260.

[9] See Hilaire Belloc, *The Servile State* (Indianapolis, IN: Liberty Fund, 1977); Wendell Berry, *What Are People For?* (San Francisco, CA: North Point Press, 1990); and John Crowe Ransom et al., *I'll Take My Stand. The South and the Agrarian Tradition, by Twelve Southerners* (Baton Rouge and London: Louisiana University Press, 1930, 1958).

of virtue from extinction. In the footsteps of Benedict of Nursia, they will strive to weather the social and cultural storms gathering in the "post family" era. In the midst of mounting disorder, they will seek to live in faithfulness to the natural order and the divine commands, holding to the promise of salvation.

Index

176   INDEX

allowance programs, 50; wage
experiment, 6; welfare laws
and, 21, 22; and work, 166; in
year 2000, 150. *See also* Household
Family Action Plan, 134
Family and Society (Zimmerman), 168
Family wage: in Australia, 39;
and family size, 41; labor unions and, 37–38; 53; moraliz-
ing, 43; New Dealers on, 48;
nongovernmental, 35; Roman
Catholics and, 35–37; and Social Security system, 49; triumph of, 51. *See also* Wages
Family wages: AFL-CIO defense
of, 60; deconstruction of,
61–62; grow in popularity, 161
"Fannie Mae", 66, 68, 69, 75
Farnham, Marynia, 56
Federal Council of Churches, 96, 97
Federal Housing Administration:
in 1970s, 81, 82; and construction boom, 69, 71; cultural bias
of, 163; guidelines of, 75–76;
mortgage ceilings, 78; as
revolutionary, 65
Federal housing project, 73
Federal National Mortgage Association. *See* "Fannie Mae"
Feld, M. D., 127
Female. *See* Women
Feminism: and Darwinism, 140;
and home economics, 149, 156;
liberal versus social, 161; on
marriage, 151; and sex differences, 123
Fertility: Catholic, 103, 106, 161,
164; of college women, 159; in
colonial America, 13; declines,
160; home economists on, 155;
Jews and, 94; Mormons and,
93, 105, 107

FHA. *See* Federal Housing Ad-
ministration
Fiske, George Walter, 95
Fliegelman, Jay, 9
Foote, Nelson, 67
Fourteenth Amendment: equal
protection of, 22; and mar-
riage, 23; and Tenth Amend-
ment, 20, 23, 160
France, 39, 50
Frederick, Christine, 145, 146
Fuchs, Victor, 54
Future Homemakers of America,
153

Gallaway, Lowell, 22
Gates, Thomas, Jr., 122
Gender roles, 2
GI insurance, 71
Gilman, Charlotte Perkins,
140–43; Beecher and, 141, 143;
and capitalism, 141; and Future
Homemakers of America, 153;
philosophic framework of, 140;
on professional cleaners, 142;
reworking of, 166; and social
change, 142; on women in
labor, 156
"Ginnie Mae", 78
Gompers, Samuel, 37
Government National Mortgage
Association. *See* "Ginnie Mae"
Grant, Charles, 8–9
Grant, Heber J., 93
Great Britain, 42
Greeley, Andrew M., 104
Gregory, Lou Allen, 145
Greven, Philip, Jr., 12
Groves, Ernest R., 96
Guttmacher, Alan, 100

Hall, Olive, 147
Healy, James, 35